Kennedy Center
Performing Artists
Cookbook

Kennedy Center Performing Artists Cookbook

A Collection of
favorite recipes from artists
who have appeared at the Center

In addition menus and recipes
for theatregoers prepared by
Mrs. Dwight D. Eisenhower
Mrs. Aristotle Onassis
Mrs. Lyndon B. Johnson
Mrs. Alice Roosevelt Longworth
and
Mrs. Richard M. Nixon

ACKNOWLEDGMENTS

I am especially grateful to Mrs. Eugene Carusi, of the National Council of Friends, who helped and urged me forward in this endeavor and who never wavered in her support when I lagged behind; to Helen Frazer who took time off from her own job to type and edit and "office manage" the project; to my friends who helped test the recipes night after night, especially CiCi Howells; and to my husband who has sampled many of the recipes in this book—occasionally unwillingly; and also to my fellow staff workers at the Friends and at the Center itself who were always available to answer questions. And finally to Mrs. Polk Guest, Chairman of the Friends who had the idea in the first place and last but not least finally found me a desk!

Ann Terry Pincus
Editor

Edited by Ann Terry Pincus
Jacket cover and book designed by Rochelle Udell
Cover drawing by Philippe Weisbecker

FOREWORD

On behalf of the Trustees of the Kennedy Center, I would like to take this opportunity to thank the distinguished artists who have contributed to this project.

Many years ago when the John F. Kennedy Center for the Performing Arts existed only in blueprints, the Trustees strongly emphasized that it should be designed to be artistically perfect both for the performers and the audience. The great reception that the Center has received since its opening has proven that we were successful in this task. The audiences have far exceeded our most optimistic dreams and practically all of the artists who have performed at the Center have praised its facilities.

Not only are we indebted to those fine artists who have made our success possible with brilliant performances at the Center, but we are also very grateful to them for allowing us to include their favorite recipes in our Kennedy Center Cookbook. Since cooking is an art of itself, it is only reasonable to assume that the contributions of these talented people should provide the reader with great gastronomic pleasures.

Roger L. Stevens
Chairman of the Board of Trustees
John F. Kennedy Center

INTRODUCTION

The Friends of the Kennedy Center was started in 1966 by the Trustees of the Center. We have built up a membership of nearly 10,000 members from all over the country. As the Friends started before the Center was built, projects had to be embarked on that not only brought the Center to people's attention but showed its national and bipartisan aspect.

First came the Tom Sawyer fence: Under Senator Leverett Saltonstall and Mrs. Cyrus Vance, children from 48 states and 27 foreign countries, between the ages of 9 and 15 painted panels that were put around the construction site. Then came the first American College Theater Festival which we contributed to and co-ordinated in our office. It was a success and has been greatly expanded since our initial effort. While the Center was being built we manned an information trailer on the grounds, where we answered questions, showed slides of what the Center was going to look like, helped entertain distinguished visitors and arranged tours (in hard hats) for them. We maintained a Speakers Bureau ("have slides will travel" is still our slogan); sent out a newsletter; had an hour's radio program a week called "Kennedy Center Presents"; helped promote the National Opera Company which toured under the auspices of the Center and the Metropolitan Opera by arranging radio interviews with Risé Stevens, manager of the Company and the Senator and Congressman from the different parts of the country where the opera was performing.

Since the Center opened our volunteers have worked in the mail order room, run the souvenir stands, given the tours, co-ordinated the half-price ticket program, bused students in for special programs, contacted organizations and given out complimentary tickets, as well as carrying on with our Speakers Bureau, manning the volunteers office, receiving and answering complaints. We have also given money to the College Theater Festival, funded a pilot workshop program for addicts at D.C. General Hospital, contributed to a Blues Festival held at Howard University and helped bring Arthur Mitchell and his Harlem School of Dance into the schools. Since the Parks Service has moved into the Center we have been cooperating fully with them on the tours, busing special groups into the Center, developing a waiting area for tourists and working out special tourist activities such as free organ demonstrations in the Concert Hall and performances by students in the Multi Purpose Room.

The proceeds from this Cookbook will enable the Friends to contribute funds to the Center's new national education program. A national cultural center must have such a program in order to keep it from being simply a commercial venture. It is due to the performances of the fine artists presented at the Center that we *can* have such a program. And it is due to their generosity that we can have such a fine cookbook!

> Mrs. Polk Guest, Chairman, National Council of the
> Friends of the Kennedy Center

Egg and Cheese Dishes

Mr. Richmond is a young and talented concert pianist. He says the recipe below was his initiation into cooking: "Several years ago I was studying with concert pianist Earl Wild, and while visiting myself and several other fellow students he was appalled to find out that my knowledge of cooking was limited to canned soups and TV dinners . . . he investigated my meagerly stocked refrigerator and found enough ingredients to make the basic recipe. I'll never forget Earl's singing and humming as he prepared the eggs. I was so impressed that I called them 'Dynamite Eggs.' I have since added some extra ingredients to make the following recipe:"

DYNAMITE EGGS

2 pure-beef frankfurters (or chopped pieces of ham)
½ cup chopped scallions (or onions)
½ cup fresh mushrooms, chopped
2 tablespoons butter
8 large eggs

¼ cup whipping cream
½ tablespoon honey
⅓ cup mild cheese, shredded chives
salt
pepper

1

Melt the butter in a large skillet over low heat, slice the frankfurters into thin circles and brown them along with the scallions and mushrooms.

2

Beat eggs and cream until foamy. Pour them into skillet and quickly add honey, cheese, generous sprinkling of chives, salt and pepper.

3

Turn the eggs until they reach desired consistency.

Yield: four servings.

EGG AND CHEESE DISHES

"Ron"

Founding Artist Ron Townson sings with "The Fifth Dimension"
one of the country's most popular singing groups.

SPANISH EGGS

8 eggs	garlic salt
3 tablespoons butter	pepper
1 onion, chopped	chili powder
1 green pepper, chopped	salt
½ cup grated Cheddar cheese	black olives
2 tablespoons milk	paprika
6 slices crisp bacon, crumbled	parsley

1
Beat up eggs, add Cheddar cheese, bacon and milk, and set aside.
2
Saute onion and green pepper in the butter until almost done.
3
Add egg combination to onion and green pepper mixture,
add seasonings to taste, and cook until fluffy.
4
Garnish with sliced black olives, paprika and parsley.
Yield: four servings.

Lorin Maazel

Lorin Maazel, conductor of the Cleveland Orchestra is the second American in history to have taken command of one of the Nation's "Big Five" symphony orchestras.

COLD PARMESAN SOUFFLE

1 tablespoon unflavored gelatin
¼ cup cold water
½ cup hot milk
1 teaspoon onion juice
1 teaspoon lemon juice
2 cups grated Parmesan cheese

pinch of salt, curry powder, dry mustard
dash of Tabasco
1 cup heavy cream, whipped
watercress

1
First soften gelatin in cold water then dissolve in hot milk.
Combine with juices and spices and blend in Parmesan cheese.
2
Fold whipped cream into the mixture and pour into a mold rinsed with cold water.
3
Chill for three hours or until firmly set, then unmold on platter.
4
Sprinkle with grated Parmesan cheese garnished with watercress and serve with a salad course.

Yield: six servings.

EGG AND CHEESE DISHES

Mr. Hume is music editor of *The Washington Post* newspaper as well as conductor of the Georgetown University Men's Chorus. He says the recipe below is his idea "of what a great quiche can be . . . a first class hors d'oeuvre or main dish and wonderful for brunch."

QUICHE ROYALE

½ pound good ham
3 to 4 ounces Gruyere cheese
½ green pepper
2 bunches green onions
1 cup half and half
6 eggs
Worcestershire sauce
Tabasco sauce
1 tablespoon olive oil

½ tablespoon wine vinegar
pinch of salt (if the ham is sweet, not salty)
ground black pepper
paprika
2 nine-inch or 3 eight-inch pie crusts (the frozen ones from the stores work fine).

1
Cut up ham, cheese, peppers and onions in small pieces. (If you like to work ahead let ingredients marinate in oil and vinegar and other sauces overnight or for several hours, covered securely.)

2
Cook store bought pie crusts for seven or eight minutes. Heat oven to 425°.

3
Beat together eggs and half and half, stir in other ingredients and divide all into the pie crusts. Sprinkle with paprika.

4
Put quiches into 425 degree oven; after ten minutes reduce heat to 350 degrees for another twenty-five minutes.

Yield: Twelve servings as first course. Six servings as main course.

GEORGE GRIZZARD

Mr. Grizzard has appeared twice at the Kennedy Center since its opening
and has received critical acclaim for the performances in
"The Country Girl" and "The Creation of the World and other Business."
Here is what he writes about food:

"Actors are for the most part very honest people. Honesty is our business;
but on occasion some of us have been known to pilfer an idea or a walk;
a shrug or a look. When it comes to recipes, however, our dishonesty
knows no bounds. Gaye Jordan Elwell is a marvelous actress and a
brilliant cook. She stole this recipe from Mrs. Child and
improved upon it. I stole it from her."

CHEESE AND BACON RAMEQUIN

½ cup flour
2 cups cold milk
4½ tablespoons butter
½ teaspoon salt
⅛ teaspoon pepper
pinch of nutmeg

4 eggs
1½ cups Swiss cheese, coarsely
grated
1 pound crisp crumbled bacon
lightly buttered Ramequin pan

1
Place flour in heavy two and one half quart saucepan and gradually beat in
milk with a wire whisk. Stir slowly and constantly over moderately
high heat until mixture comes to a boil and becomes very thick.

2
Remove from heat; beat in three and one half tablespoons of butter,
seasonings, and one by one, the eggs. Then beat in the cheese.

3
Turn one half of the mixture into the buttered ramequin. Scatter bacon
evenly over surface and cover with the remaining mixture. Scatter more
Swiss cheese over all and dot with one tablespoon of butter.

4
Preheat oven to 400°.

5
Bake in upper third of oven for about thirty-five minutes. The ramequin
is done when it has puffed to double its height and is beautifully browned.
Serve at once, as it will sink as it cools. Accompany with green salad,
French bread and dry white wine.

Yield: four servings.

QUICK QUICHE LORRAINE

Pastry:

1¾ cups flour	¼ cup water
¼ pound unsalted butter	½ teaspoon salt
3 tablespoons vegetable oil	pinch sugar

1

In a large bowl, using a fork, combine flour, butter and oil. Slowly add water, sugar and salt. Continue to work the dough with your hands rather rapidly (as it tends to soften). When the dough feels smooth and elastic, form a ball, cover and refrigerate for about ten minutes.

2

Preheat oven to 350 degrees. Roll out dough on wooden board, then line a nine and one half inch pie shell with the dough, pressing quickly with your fingers from the center of the shell up to the sides. The sides of the shell should be covered more thickly than the bottom. Flute the edges of the shell with the dull side of a knife.

Filling:

½ pound bacon	1⅓ cups Swiss cheese, grated
3 eggs	½ teaspoon nutmeg
1½ cups light cream	pinch pepper

1

Cut bacon into one-inch pieces, fry until crisp and drain on paper towel.

2

Combine remaining ingredients and stir with a fork.

3

Put bacon in bottom of shell. Then add cream mixture. Sprinkle more nutmeg on top.

4

Bake in a 350 degree oven thirty-five to forty minutes until golden brown. Yield: six servings as a first course.

Jaime and Ruth Laredo

The Laredos appeared in concert together at the Kennedy Center with
Mr. Laredo playing the violin and Mrs. Laredo, the piano.

RUTH LAREDO'S EASY QUICHE LORRAINE

(CRUST)

1 cup flour
1 stick butter
3 ounces cream cheese

1
Mix together. Form into a ball and chill in refrigerator for about an hour.

2
Roll out and place into small pie shell. Bake at 450 degrees for ten minutes
pierceing with fork or until slightly brown.

(FILLING)

1 pint light cream
½ cup grated Cheddar cheese
2 eggs, beaten
½ pound fried bacon, crumbled
salt
pepper

1
Scald the cream in a sauce pan (do not boil it). Add the grated
cheese, eggs, bacon, salt and pepper to taste.

2
Pour into baked pie shell and bake for half an hour to forty-five
minutes at 325 degrees.

Yield: eight servings as first course.

Benita Valente

Benita Valente, the operatic lyric soprano, has given us this recipe.

MOZZARELLA IN CARROZZA
(Cheese and prosciutto ham sandwich)

8 slices white bread
4 slices mozzarella cheese
2 eggs, beaten
1 tablespoon butter

1 tablespoon oil
4 slices prosciutto ham
parsley

1
Choose firm textured white bread and remove crust with a sharp knife.

2
Cut mozzarella in one-half inch thick slices. Place a slice of mozzarella on a slice of bread, place a slice of prosciutto over the cheese and cover with another slice of bread. If necessary, trim bread slices to fit the cheese slice.

3
Beat eggs in a pie plate. Dip each sandwich in the eggs so that all surfaces are thoroughly coated, but not soggy.

4
Place oil and butter in a heavy skillet and when hot, but not smoking, place sandwiches in it. When golden on one side, turn sandwiches carefully with spatula and brown other side.

5
Remove and let sit on absorbent paper a minute. Garnish with parsley and serve.
Yield: four servings.

Soups

Lorin Maazel

Lorin Maazel, conductor of the Cleveland Orchestra, is the second American in history to have taken command of one of the nation's "Big Five" Symphony orchestras.

AVOCADO YOGHURT SOUP

2 cups avocados
2 cups yoghurt
1½ cups beef stock

3 teaspoons lime juice
2 teaspoons onion juice
1 teaspoon chili powder

1
Mash avocados with silver fork to make two cups.
2
Force through sieve with yoghurt, beef stock, lime juice, onion juice and chili powder.
3
Chill thoroughly and serve.
Yield: four servings.

SOUPS

[signature: Michael York]

Mr. York, a young and upcoming film and stage actor who starred in Tennessee Williams' controversial play "Out Cry" when it played at the Kennedy Center, passes his recipe to us with the following comments: "One of the few genuinely philanthropic services to mankind I can perform is to pass on to the uninitiated the recipe for this life-giving and life-enhancing soup. It was formulated by Dr. Henry Bieler, the celebrated California nutritionalist. Beware! Once supped never substituted!"

BIELER BROTH

8 large zucchini, cut into short lengths
8 stalks celery, cut into two-inch lengths
2 packages frozen string beans (or one pound, fresh)

1 tablespoon unsalted butter
1 handful parsley, cut up
1½ cups distilled water (if you are not a purist you may substitute chicken broth and add salt as well)

1
Cut ends off zucchini and place with celery, string beans and water in pot. Cover. Cook until tender.

2
Place contents in a blender, add butter and parsley, blend and eat "and live!" adds Mr. York.

Yield: four servings generously.

Kenneth Riegel

Opera tenor Kenneth Riegel has contributed this delicious soup to our Cookbook.

PENNSYLVANIA DUTCH CORN CHOWDER

4 slices bacon
1 tablespoon celery, finely chopped
1 tablespoon green pepper,
  finely chopped
2 potatoes, peeled and chopped
3 tomatoes, peeled and chopped
2 cups corn kernels,
  fresh from the cob

1 pint milk
1 pint light cream
1 cup water
salt
pepper

1

Chop bacon and place in pan to brown. Add minced celery, pepper and onion, fry together until bacon is brown.

2

Add corn and saute together for three minutes. Add the chopped vegetables and water. Cover and cook slowly for thirty minutes.

3

Add milk and cream and heat to boiling again. Add chopped parsley.

Yield: four servings.

Kenneth Pasmanick

Kenneth Pasmanick is the First Bassoonist with the National Symphony.

WATER CRESS SOUP

2 cups water cress, tightly packed   1 teaspoon salt
½ pound lean beef, finely chopped   3 cups chicken broth
1 tablespoon butter   3 cups water
1 tablespoon soy sauce   drop of sesame seed oil
1 teaspoon cooking oil

1
Wash and stem the watercress.
2
Dice the beef. Lightly saute in butter until cooked (about 2 minutes). Then season with soy sauce and oil and salt and let stand about thirty minutes.
3
Bring chicken broth and water to a boil, add the water cress, stir well and bring the soup to a boil again.
4
Add a drop of sesame oil and the seasoned beef. Stir thoroughly and serve very hot.
Yield: six to eight servings.
Note: Add more water cress and strips of beef and it turns into a main dish, served with hot mustard.

Evelyn Swarthout

Miss Evelyn Swarthout, the concert pianist, has given us a delicious yet healthy soup.

YOGHURT SOUP WITH MINT

¼ cup pearl barley
6 cups chicken broth
2 tablespoons onion, minced
½ cup fresh mint, finely chopped

3 cups unflavored yoghurt
¾ teaspoon salt
pepper to taste

1
Cover barley with cold water and soak overnight.
2
After it has soaked, drain and rinse well and put into medium-sized sauce pan with the broth and onion; bring to a boil, then lower heat and simmer fifteen minutes or until tender.
3
Remove from heat, add mint, cool to room temperature. Add yoghurt, stir until smooth. Add salt and pepper to taste and serve very cold in chilled soup plates.
Yield: eight servings.

Rice and Pasta Dishes

Carla Fracci

Miss Fracci, a prima ballerina with the American Ballet Theatre, has performed often before delighted Washington audiences at the Center.

RISOTTO ALLA MILANESE

1 cup uncooked rice
¼ cup onions, finely chopped
¼ cup butter
1 tablespoon olive oil
3 cups chicken broth

1 chicken bouillon cube
¼ teaspoon saffron
2 tablespoons hot water
¼ cup grated Parmesan cheese
salt to taste

1
In a heavy saucepan, melt the butter with the olive oil. Add the onion, allowing it to fry slightly, add the rice and cook until slightly brown stirring with a fork.

2
Stir in the broth, slowly, add the bouillon cube. Allow the rice to simmer for a few minutes, covered, as it absorbs the broth.

3
Dissolve the saffron in the hot water, add to the rice. Be sure not to overcook the rice; the entire procedure should not take more than fifteen minutes. Turn off the heat and add the grated cheese.

4
Let the mixture sit for ten minutes, but serve while still quite warm.
Yield: four servings. Miss Fracci adds, "This amount should serve four people, but all depends on how much everyone wants to eat as a first course!"

Maurice Peress

Conductor Maurice Peress, the Music Director of the Corpus Christi Symphony, conducted Bernstein's "Mass" at the Kennedy Center opening and was the Music Director of "Candide" when it played at the Center.

RISOTTO MILANESE

2½ cups rice
 5 tablespoons butter
 5 tablespoons olive oil
 2 tablespoons chopped beef
    marrow
 3 small onions, chopped

 2 cloves garlic, minced (optional)
2½ quarts chicken stock, boiling
pinch of saffron
 2 cups Parmesan cheese
 ¼ cup Madeira

1
Melt the butter in a heavy saucepan, add oil and beef marrow. Add chopped onions and the garlic if you are using it and saute until the onions are pale gold.
2
Stir in the raw rice over moderate heat and cook for five minutes, stirring constantly. Add the boiling chicken stock about a cup at a time. As the rice absorbs the liquid add the next cup, stirring frequently.
3
Dilute the saffron with a little chicken stock and add to the rice. The rice should cook covered for at least fifteen minutes until all liquid has been absorbed.
4
Before serving, lightly stir in the cheese and a few small lumps of butter. Yield: eight to ten servings.

Pearl Bailey

Founding Artist Pearl Bailey made her start in show business in Washington, D.C. more than thirty years ago and when she appeared at the Center the town showed it still loves her. The recipe below was taken from her own cookbook *Pearl's Kitchen*. About this recipe Miss Bailey says, "Nobody ever has a little bit of my macaroni and cheese . . . (It) is my most famous personal recipe . . . no matter how closely you follow my instructions, your macaroni and cheese will never taste exactly like mine, but we'll hope."

MACARONI AND CHEESE

2 pounds macaroni ("I prefer elbow")
2 sticks butter
1 pound sharp Cheddar cheese

2 cups milk
salt
pepper

1
Boil macaroni according to package directions until it is three-quarters done. Then run cold water over it and wash away all the milky whiteners. "There's nothing worse, you know, than sticky macaroni."

2
Season macaroni with salt, pepper and butter. Then chop cheese into small hunks and spread it over the macaroni.

3
Put them into a roasting pan and "pour milk right up to the top of the macaroni."

4
Slide the whole thing into the oven at 350 degrees (do not cover) and cook it until the cheese starts to melt. At this point take it out and stir with a spoon so that cheese goes all the way through the macaroni.

5
"Then I shove it back in the oven (still no cover) and let that baby just get bubbly brown until I'm sure the cheese is fully melted all the way to the bottom."

Yield: ten servings.

"Now of course you can serve it hot. Then the next day it's better and the third day it's better still . . . that's all there is to it, and there's nothing I would rather put in front of guests than my macaroni and cheese."

Tony Bennett

It has been said about Founding Artist Tony Bennett that when he
sings a song it stays sung. He brings out the best in a song
as his mother brings out the best in lasagna.

TONY BENNETT'S MOTHER'S LASAGNA

2 pounds ground beef
1 pound Italian sausage
(without skin)
1½ large cans tomatoes (seeded
and strained)
1 small can tomato paste

1 large can ricotta cheese
4 cups grated cheese (preferably
not Mozzarella)
5 raw eggs
2 packages lasagna
2 tablespoons cooking oil

1
Crumble ground beef and sausage and brown together without oil.

2
Brown tomato paste in separate pan.

3
Combine meats, tomato paste and tomatoes, salt and pepper and
cook slowly two hours on top of stove uncovered.

4
Cook lasagna with oil and water until *al dente,* strain, and rinse in
cold water and drain.

5
Beat the eggs into the ricotta.

6
Grease two, two-quart baking dishes and put layer of sauce, then lasagna,
then ricotta, then grated cheese and so on in basket weave pattern
until all is used up.

7
Bake at 350° for forty-five minutes.
Yield: 12 to 14 servings.

Leonard Pennario

Leonard Pennario, concert pianist, writes that "Although I very much appreciate superb cuisine, and this is one of the pleasures of making concert tours throughout the world, I myself am a disaster in the kitchen, not being able to boil water . . . however, I would like to make a contribution so am sending you the recipe for one of my favorite dishes."

LINGUINE WITH CLAM SAUCE

¼ cup olive oil
¼ cup butter
3 tablespoons parsley, finely chopped
1 clove garlic, mashed
¼ teaspoon salt
⅛ teaspoon pepper

3 drops of liquid hot pepper seasoning
¼ teaspoon oregano leaves, crumbled
3 to 4 dozen small hard-shell clams, washed well
2 tablespoons water
6 ounces of hot cooked linguine

1
Heat the olive oil and butter in a frying pan. Add parsley and garlic and saute for one to two minutes.
2
Add salt, pepper, hot pepper seasoning and oregano. Simmer gently, stir for about ten minutes, then reduce heat to keep warm.
3
Place clams and water into a heavy pan. Cover and simmer just until clams open (five to ten minutes). Then pluck whole clams from the shells and put into the sauce. Strain clam juices from bottom of pan, and add juice to the sauce. Reheat and serve over the hot linguine.
Yield: six servings.

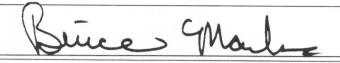

Bruce Marks, long a principle with the American Ballet Theatre and now with the Royal Danish Ballet, writes about his recipe, "It is not exactly a dish for those of you who are trying to 'hold that line.' If, however, you think that you have trouble just remember that most of our friends are dancers and I'm sure that I have been cursed by more than one ballerina for serving this 'forbidden fruit.' If there is anything dancers like to do as much as dance it is eat."

SPAGHETTI A LA CARBONARA

1 pound spaghetti	8 strips bacon
1 pint medium cream	1 cup Parmesan cheese
2 eggs	salt
2 additional egg yolks	pepper

1
Mix the cream, eggs and egg yolks, adding four tablespoons of Parmesan cheese. Set aside.
2
Cut up bacon into one inch pieces and grill in a large pan.
3
Boil the spaghetti in four quarts of water with salt and a drop of cooking oil. Make sure pasta is firm but not hard (al dente).
4
Drain spaghetti thoroughly and add to the bacon. Using medium heat toss the spaghetti until any remaining water has disappeared and then add egg mixture.
5
Continue tossing for a few minutes making sure the heat is not too strong. Add salt and plenty of fresh ground pepper and serve with more cheese.
Yield: four servings.

RICE AND PASTA DISHES

Julius Rudel

Mr. Rudel, in addition to being the director of the New York City Opera, is a father of the Kennedy Center. As Music Director of the Center he has nourished its beginning and helped it to grow.

SPAGHETTI ALLA CREMA

4 tablespoons shallots, chopped
2 cloves garlic, crushed
2 tablespoons butter
1 cup beef bouillon
1 cup dry white wine
½ pint heavy cream
14 ounces spaghetti

salt
pepper
1 pound fresh mushrooms, diced
2 sprigs parsley, minced
½ tablespoon butter
lemon peel

1

Place shallots, garlic and butter in pan, cook until shallots and garlic are translucent; add bouillon and cook slowly until liquid is reduced to half; add wine and cook again uncovered until fluid is reduced again to half; add cream and bring to a boil. Add salt and pepper to taste and it is ready to serve.

2

If mushrooms are desired, cook them slowly in butter, parsley and lemon peel.

3

Cook spahgetti until *al dente;* add sauce, with mushrooms on top.
Yield: eight servings.

SPAGHETTI WITH GARLIC AND HERBS

4 cloves garlic, crushed
4 sprigs parsley, minced
2 teaspoons fresh basil, chopped
  (if available) or ½ teaspoon, dried
oregano, rosemary, thyme to
  taste

2 tablespoons butter
2 tablespoons olive oil
salt
pepper
8 ounces spaghetti
Parmesan cheese

1

Place garlic, parsley and other herbs in pan with melted butter and olive oil. Cook slowly until garlic is golden.

2

Meanwhile cook spaghetti *al dente,* add sauce and serve with grated Parmesan cheese.
Yield: eight servings.
Mr. Rudel suggests this light pasta dish as a delicious accompaniment to chicken or veal. His recipe for chicken can be found in the poultry section.

RICE AND PASTA DISHES

Rae Allen

Miss Rae Allen, outstanding singing comedienne , one of the leads in the Kennedy Center production of the musical "Candide" has sent us a recipe for "fast" spaghetti sauce

FAST SPAGHETTI SAUCE

1 clove garlic, chopped
1 medium onion, chopped
2 tablespoons cooking oil
1 pound lean beef
2 medium cans tomatoes

½ can tomato paste
dash of oregano
1 tablespoon fresh parsley
salt
pepper

1
Saute garlic and onion in oil, until transparent, add beef, then add tomatoes tomato paste, oregano, parsley and salt and pepper to taste.
2
Cover and cook for forty-five minutes. Serve over spaghetti.
Yield: four servings.

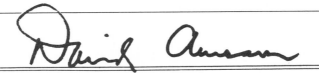

Composer-conductor David Amram has been remarkably prolific having composed many chamber works, a wind symphony, cantatas, operas and scores for both plays and films.

TEN-MINUTE ITALIAN SPAGHETTI

2 pounds spaghetti
2 tins anchovy fillets
3 tablespoons olive oil
2 tins tomato paste

3 cloves garlic, chopped
2 tins water (tomato paste size)
½ teaspoon pepper
1 teaspoon oregano

1
Cook spaghetti in boiling, salted water.
2
While it is cooking make the following sauce: Mix anchovy fillets with olive oil in frying pan. Mash with a spoon and add tomato paste, garlic, water, pepper and oregano.
3
Cook over fast fire for ten minutes and pour over spaghetti.
Yield: four servings.

RICE AND PASTA DISHES

Cannonball Adderley

A Founding Artist of the Center the inimitable Mr. Adderley, King of the alto saxophone, is also a gourmand. He earned his nickname from his voracious appetite after a friend saw him consume several breakfasts. He called him the "cannibal" which in time became "Cannonball."

"CANNONBALL" ADDERLEY'S SPAGHETTI SAUCE

½ pint clam juice
1 tablespoon olive oil
½ pint dry white wine
18 raw clams in shell
½ pint eastern oysters
¼ pound small scallops
½ pound raw cleaned shrimp

¼ pound crab meat
1 clove garlic, crushed
¼ tablespoon accent seasoning
2 tablespoons dill weed
salt
pepper
1 package thin spaghetti

1
Put garlic and oil in skillet. Add clams and clam juice, cover and steam until clams open.

2
Add oysters, when they begin to curl, add scallops, crab meat and wine; bring to a boil.

2
Add shrimp, cover pot, immediately turn off heat. Let stand until shrimp turns pink.

4
Add seasonings to taste and serve over thin spaghetti.
Yield: six servings.

Shellfish and Fresh Water Fish

Pernell Roberts

Pernell Roberts, who appeared in "Captain Brassbound's Conversion" at the Kennedy Center, loves to cook as well as act and sing. He says this recipe for Cioppino is really wonderful. "I have had friends call my house and ask if they could please be invited to dinner the next time we make Cioppino." We agree with Mr. Roberts' friends.

CIOPPINO

5 big leeks	salt
1½ bunches parsley	pepper
1 stalk celery	paprika for color
3 green peppers	1 cup red wine
5 carrots	juice of two lemons
½ pound fresh or dried mushrooms	½ cup Parmesan cheese
12 pips of garlic	3 crabs, cracked
2 cups olive oil	30 mussels, scrubbed
peel from one orange	30 littleneck clams, scrubbed
1½ teaspoons oregano	2 pounds shrimp
2 teaspoons fennel seed	3 lobster tails (this can be omitted
6 bay leaves	if you are on a budget)
3 fifteen-ounce cans Italian-style	2 pounds solid type filleted fish,
tomatoes	cut into two-inch cubes
8 ounces clam broth	

1
Assemble the greens (leeks, parsley, celery, peppers, carrots, mushrooms and garlic) and chop very fine. ("It really is worth the trouble and will make a smoother sauce later.")

2
Pour olive oil into largest pot or roasting pan you have and saute above vegetables in oil until tender and transparent.

3
Add orange peel (do not chop), oregano, fennel seed, bay leaves, tomatoes, clam broth, salt, pepper and paprika. Stir well. Pour in red wine and lemon juice.

4
Cover, cook on very low flame for one hour, stirring every ten minutes or so. For last twenty minutes of cooking, stir in Parmesan cheese. When done, discard bay leaves and orange peel.

5
Pour sauce from roaster into large pot temporarily. Lay clams and mussels on bottom of roaster pan. Next place in the raw shellfish. Over this lay fish chunks. Lastly, put crab pieces over fish. Pour sauce over the whole thing. *Don't stir.* Cover roaster.

6
Cook stew on low flame for one half hour. Do not stir. When done, serve as you would a casserole, making sure each serving gets all kinds of fish.

Yield: twelve servings.

Note: "It is great with lots of Italian bread and you will need lots of napkins, discard plates and generous glasses of red wine."

Leonard Bernstein

Mr. Bernstein, world-famous composer and conductor, created "Mass," a Theatre Piece for Singers, Players and Dancers, for the opening of the Kennedy Center on September 8, 1971.

CHUPE
(Seafood Casserole)

3 six-ounce loaves of French bread
5 cups milk
1 quart water
1 tablespoon salt
1 bay leaf
2 pounds scallops (washed)
1 pound shrimp (peeled and cleaned)
2 tablespoons paprika

1 teaspoon Tabasco
1¼ sticks butter
½ teaspoon oregano
¼ teaspoon black pepper
1 onion (sliced)
2 large lobster tails
½ pound crab meat
¼ pound mozzarella cheese
4 hard-boiled eggs
Parmesan cheese

1
Cut bread into slices and soak in milk.
2
Bring water with salt and bay leaf to a boil. Add scallops and cook about three minutes. Reserve scallops, add shrimp and cook until pink. Remove shrimp.
3
Add about one and one-half cups of the broth to bread mixture. Add paprika, Tabasco and four tablespoons of butter. Mix well and sieve or run through a food mill.
4
Add enough water to remaining broth to make about three quarts. Add oregano, black pepper and onion and bring to a boil. Add lobster tails and boil about eight minutes. Cool lobster, shell and cut into one-inch slices.
5
Discard broth, wash pot and place in it all seafood, bread puree, mozzarella and three tablespoons of butter. Mix.
6
Spread half of the mixture in two shallow three-quart casseroles. Add eggs cut in wedges, and remaining seafood mixture. Sprinkle with Parmesan cheese and dot with remaining bits of butter.
7
Bake in pre-heated hot oven (400 degrees) until golden brown— about twenty minutes.
Yield: Ten servings

Spiro Malas

Mr. Malas sings bass with the New York City Opera.

CRAB CAKE PUFFS

.

1 pound crab meat (Chesapeake Bay blue is best)
½ cup soft bread crumbs
3 tablespoons parsley, chopped
2 eggs
1 teaspoon dry mustard
1 teaspoon Worcestershire sauce

mayonnaise to moisten
2 cups flour
1 teaspoon salt
1 teaspoon seafood seasoning
½ teaspoon white pepper
pinch baking soda
2 cups cooking oil

1
Mix crab meat with bread crumbs, parsley, one egg, dry mustard and Worcestershire sauce and add enough mayonnaise to moisten.

2
Shape the crab mixture into balls about the size of golf balls.

3
Combine flour, one egg, salt and other seasonings with enough water to make a thick batter.

4
Dip each crab cake in the batter and deep fry in hot fat until browned and puffed.

Yield: four servings.

SHELLFISH AND FRESH WATER FISH

Martina Arroyo

Founding Artist Martina Arroyo, one of the Metropolitan Opera's top American sopranos and a reigning voice in the opera world has talents in the world of cuisine as well.

CRAB DISH

⅓ cup chopped onions
⅓ cup chopped green peppers
⅓ cup chopped celery
2 cloves of garlic
1 bouillon cube (chicken or beef)
1 pound fresh crabmeat (carefully picked)

2 tablespoons olive oil
½ cup Parmesan cheese
½ cup breadcrumbs
Tabasco sauce
salt
pepper

1
Heat olive oil with garlic cloves. Add onions, green peppers and celery. Saute slowly until light brown.
2
Add parsley, bouillon cube, Tabasco sauce and salt and pepper to taste.
3
At the last minute toss in fresh crabmeat and mix well.
4
Fill mixture into individual shells and sprinkle grated Parmesan cheese and breadcrumbs over top.
5
Bake in medium hot oven until cheese is melted brown. Serve piping hot.
Yield: Six servings.
(This is suitable as a first course or with a green salad as a light lunch.)

Leontyne Price

Miss Price, the great operatic soprano, was honored by President Johnson who said, "Her singing has brought light to her land."

CRAB MEAT IMPERIAL CASSEROLE

1 large green pepper, diced
2 pimentos, diced
½ teaspoon salt
½ teaspoon freshly ground white pepper
1 tablespoon dry mustard

3 tablespoons mayonnaise
2 eggs, lightly beaten
3 tablespoons sherry
2 pounds fresh back fin lump crab meat
paprika

1
Preheat oven to 350 degrees.
2
Mix the diced pepper and pimentos. Add salt, pepper, mustard, mayonnaise, eggs and two tablespoons of sherry; mix.
3
Carefully fold the crab meat into the pepper mixture so as not to break the lumps of crab.
4
Add the remaining tablespoon of sherry and place in a buttered casserole. Coat the top of the casserole with a thin layer of mayonnaise and sprinkle with paprika. Bake fifteen minutes.
Yield: six servings.

Fran Stevens

Miss Fran Stevens starred in the revival of Sigmund Romberg's "The Student Prince" at the Center. Her recipe is from her father's cookbook, *Eat, Drink and be Merry in Maryland.*

OYSTER LOAF

1 Vienna loaf of bread
1 quart raw oysters and liquid
1 tablespoon chopped parsley
½ cup cream

2 drops Tabasco
butter
salt
pepper

1
Cut an oblong slice from the upper crust of a Vienna loaf of bread. Then scoop out the crumbs from the inside.
2
Spread the casing with butter and fill with one quart of raw oysters. Reserve oyster liquid.
3
Add chopped parsley, cream, plenty of butter, pepper, salt and Tabasco sauce. Put on top crust.
4
Put in baking dish and pour oyster liquid over it.
5
Cover and bake for twenty minutes basting often with the liquid.
6
Slice and serve hot.
Yield: twelve servings, generously.

Justino Diaz

Metropolitan Opera bass, Justino Diaz was the original Count Cenci in Ginastera's "Beatrix Cenci" at the Kennedy Center.

PAELLA

2 chicken breasts split
4 pork sausages cut in half
1 dozen clams
1 dozen mussels
4 rock lobster tails in shells
1 large ripe tomato, peeled and chopped
2 cloves garlic, minced
½ teaspoon paprika

½ cup shelled peas
2 cups uncooked rice
1 package frozen artichoke hearts
4 teaspoons olive oil
5 cups boiling chicken broth (or water)
pinch of saffron
salt
pepper

1
Brown chicken and sausages in olive oil over high heat in heavy skillet. Add tomato, garlic, peas, paprika, artichoke hearts and allow them to brown lightly. Add rice and cook until rice begins to brown.

2
Add salt, saffron (dissolved in a little boiling water) and the broth which must be boiling. Stir briefly and cook over high heat for five minutes. Lower heat and cook fifteen minutes covered.

3
Separately cook mussels and clams in water to cover until shells open. Drain and discard one shell from each clam and mussel and add to rice mixture when rice is half cooked.

4
Garnish paella with lobster tails in their shells, brushed with melted butter.
Yield: four servings.

Lloyd Geisler

Lloyd Geisler recently retired as the Resident Conductor of the National Symphony. He suggests that his recipe below is "especially enjoyable if you are attending a concert that includes in the program Handel's 'Water Music' and/or Debussy's 'La Mer.'"

SEAFOOD NEWBURG

4 lobster tails (4 to 6 ounces each)
1 pound medium shrimp
1 pint fresh oysters
¾ pound scallops
6 tablespoons butter

4 tablespoons flour
1½ cups milk
¼ cup sherry
salt
pepper

1
Clean shrimp, remove meat from lobster tails and cut into chunks. If scallops are large, cut in half.

2
Saute lightly lobster and shrimp in two tablespoons of butter. Remove from pan. Add scallops and saute lightly and remove from pan. Add more butter if necessary and saute oysters until the edges curl. Do not overcook.

3
Make a thick white sauce by first melting four tablespoons of butter, then mix in the flour tablespoon by tablespoon. When thoroughly blended and lightly cooked, add heated milk at once and stir until thickened. Thin down with remaining liquid in pan.

4
Add the seafood and sherry and season to taste. Heat thoroughly but do not boil. Serve over cooked rice.
Yield: six to eight servings.

Robert Merrill

Metropolitan Opera baritone Robert Merrill writes that "this dish is a good one to prepare if you find yourself with unexpected company and want to do something a little different."

SEAFOOD NEWBURG

4 tablespoons butter or margarine
4 tablespoons flour
2 cups light cream
½ teaspoon salt
¼ teaspoon paprika
¼ cup dry sherry

2 pounds combined mixture of cooked shrimp, crabmeat, lobster and scallops, cut or flaked into bite-sized pieces. (You may use any combination of the above shellfish or omit if you wish.)
2 cups steamed rice

1

Melt butter then blend in flour. Add cream stirring constantly over medium heat until thickened and smooth. Add salt, paprika and sherry and continue to stir. Do not boil.

2

Add cooked seafood and heat to serving temperature and serve over steamed rice.

Yield: five to six servings.

Dizzie Gillespie

Dizzie Gillespie, often described as the father of modern jazz, is a Founding Artist of the Kennedy Center as well as a great breakfast cook.

"BREAKFAST A LA DIZZIE"

8 slices bacon
1 large onion (cut or sliced)
1 large can red or pink Alaskan salmon

1 egg yolk
2 cups water
1 cup Hominy grits

1
Cook bacon in frying pan; when bacon is done, put the onions on top of the bacon and simmer for approximately five minutes (or when onions are soft).

2
Put can of salmon into large bowl (be sure to pick bones out), add egg yolk and beat up.

3
Pour contents of bowl into frying pan with bacon and onions and turn fire down low. Let cook very slowly with top on pan until juicy.

4
Put water in separate pot and boil. Add grits to boiling water and cook for fifteen minutes; meanwhile stirring grits to keep from getting lumpy.

5
Put Hominy grits on plate and pour contents of frying pan on top and serve.
"UM . . . UM . . . UM . . . UM . . . UM . . . UM . . .", writes Dizzy.
Yield: three people.

SHELLFISH AND FRESH WATER FISH

Maurice Evans

Mr. Evans, one of Britain's most brilliant acting experts, narrated Roberto Gerhard's interpretation of Albert Camus' "The Plague", accompanied by the National Symphony. About his recipe he writes, "These days of astronomical food costs call for recipes which avoid wrecking the weekly budget. Here is one which my theatrical friends devour with relish...I always have one in the freezer for the emergency lunch or supper."

SALMON MOUSSE MAURICE

1 can red salmon (7 ½ to 8 ounce)	1 teaspoon lemon juice
½ ounce gelatin	salt
4 tablespoons cold water	pepper
1 cup unsweetened evaporated milk	1 cucumber, sliced
2 tablespoons mayonnaise	1 lemon, in wedges
	bunch of watercress
	capers

1

Place gelatin in cold water in small bowl standing in a pan of hot water and stir until completely dissolved and clear.

2

Drain salmon and remove skin and bones. Blend, at low speed, the milk for thirty seconds. Add salmon, gelatin, lemon juice and mayonnaise, salt and pepper to taste. Blend all together on low for thirty seconds.

3

Turn into wetted six-inch mould or cake tin and chill until firm.

4

To serve, loosen edges with a wet knife and dip tin in hot water until mousse can be shaken out on a damp plate.

5

Decorate with cucumbers, lemon wedges, watercress, capers or what ever you prefer. Serve with fresh green salad and/or diced cucumber in sour cream.

Yield: four servings for summer luncheon or six to eight servings for first course if set in small plain moulds.

Founding Artist B. B. King, the gracious and prolific blues singer, also loves to cook. "You can learn the blues like you can learn to be a good cook, but in order to really groove with either, you got to have that extra feeling for it, and that can't be learned."

SALMON (OR MACKEREL) CROQUETTES

1 large can salmon (or mackerel)
½ cup water
2 eggs
½ cup flour

2 tablespoons minced onion
pinch of red pepper
pinch of black pepper
salt to taste
1 cup cooking oil

1
Cut and mash up the fish. Add water and mix. Then mix in the eggs. Add flour and mix again. Stir in onions and peppers.
2
Make into patties and fry in hot oil in frying pan until done.
Yield: four to six servings.

Geoffrey Sumner

Mr. Sumner appeared in "The Jockey Club Stakes," where his comedy acting talent was happily evident to all. He calls the recipe below "one of my favorite after-the-show bits of nonsense."

SCAMPI POTOMAC

1 package frozen shrimp   ¼ cup milk
1 tin Newburg sauce   1 shot glass cognac

Boil the shrimp, mix with the milk, heat Newburg sauce, and warmed cognac "and you have a delicacy fit for a lord...."
Yield: four servings.

Royes Fernandez

Royes Fernandez, a principal dancer with the American Ballet Theatre, was born and raised in New Orleans and says "my cooking inspiration originates with my mother, who was of French descent and a marvelous chef."

SHRIMP CREOLE

4 tablespoons butter
1 large onion, chopped
2 cloves garlic, crushed
1 green pepper, chopped
½ cup celery, chopped
2 tablespoons flour
2 large tomatoes, peeled and chopped or 1 cup chopped canned tomatoes

½ cup water
1 sprig thyme
1 bay leaf
2 pounds shrimp, shelled and deveined
salt
pepper
chopped parsley

1
Melt butter in a large skillet, add onion, garlic, green pepper and celery, and saute ten minutes.
2
Sprinkle flour over vegetables stirring to combine. Gradually add tomatoes and water stirring constantly. Add thyme and bayleaf; bring to a boil and simmer covered for thirty minutes.
3
Add shrimp and simmer covered fifteen minutes more. Add salt and pepper to taste. Garnish with chopped parsley and serve over rice.
Yield: ten servings.

Zubin Mehta

Zubin Mehta, the Music Director of the Los Angeles Philharmonic, has contributed the recipe below which reflects his native India.

SHRIMP PATIA

1½	pounds shrimp		oil for cooking
4	large onions, minced		salt to taste
6	large tomatoes	½	teaspoon turmeric powder
8	cloves garlic	½	teaspoon ground cumin powder
4	whole green chilies	½	teaspoon cayenne pepper
½	bunch fresh green coriander	1½	tablespoons paprika
	leaves	1½	tablespoons sugar
		3	tablespoons red wine vinegar

1

Peel tomatoes and chop, saving juice as you cut. Pick coriander leaves from stems, wash and cut fine.

2

Shell shrimp, wash and boil in salted water until cooked. Drain and set aside.

3

Slit green chilies lengthwise. Mix with vinegar and sugar and set aside.

4

Heat oil and cook garlic until it turns pink in color. Add onions and cook until creamy and transparent. Add turmeric, cumin, paprika and cayenne, and let cook until brown (about five minutes) stirring all the time.

5

Add chopped tomatoes and keep stirring until the spiced onion mixture and tomatoes are well blended. Add green chilies, cover and cook over medium low fire, stirring now and again, so that mixture will not stick or burn at the bottom of pan.

6

Keep cooking until all liquid is absorbed. After the first ten minutes of cooking, keep the pan open and simmer to help liquid to diminish.

7

Add cooked shrimp, salt and stir well for a few minutes. Add chopped coriander leaves, mix well but lightly. Pour sugar and vinegar mixture over all; tilt the pan from side to side so all is covered.

8

Remove from fire and serve with yellow coconut rice.

Yield: Six servings.

Note: This can be prepared days ahead and either refrigerate or freeze.

Claire Bloom

Miss Claire Bloom appeared in Washington at the opening of the Eisenhower Theatre in Ibsen's "The Doll House." She says about her recipe, "It will make you neither strong, healthy nor wise, but it is a good light meal either before a performance if you are not too nervous to eat, or after when you are too tired to eat anything heavier."

SAUTEED SHRIMP

½ pound shrimp
½ cup celery, finely chopped
½ cup mushrooms, finely sliced
2 tablespoons soya oil
1 tablespoon soy sauce

1 clove garlic, crushed
½ cup brown rice
1½ cups boiling water
1 chicken bouillon cube

1

Saute celery, mushrooms and garlic in oil and soy sauce. When they are ready, add shrimp and cook until hot.

2

Meanwhile cook brown rice (which takes about forty-five minutes in water with dissolved bouillon cube.

3

Pour contents of frying pan over rice and serve.

Yield: two servings.

Roger L.Stevens

Roger L. Stevens, Chairman of the Board of Trustees of The Kennedy Center since 1961, has also produced more than 125 plays.

SHRIMP IN SHERRY AND TOMATO SAUCE

1½ pounds boiled shrimp
6 tablespoons butter
1 onion, finely minced
3 tablespoons parsley, chopped
5 tablespoons flour
6 fresh tomatoes, peeled and cut up

1 cup cream
6 tablespoons dry sherry
2 tablespoons Worcestershire sauce
dash of bitters

1
Brown onion in butter. Add parsley and flour.
2
Add tomatoes and let cook for five minutes. Add cream, sherry, Worcestershire sauce and bitters, and finally the shrimp.
Cook until shrimp is hot and serve.
Yield: four servings.

Merle Haggard

Singer Merle Haggard is the undisputed King of American country music.
He has given us a fine "American Country" recipe.

FILLET CATFISH

1 catfish fillet, boned and skinned
4 raw eggs
3 tablespoons honey

3 tablespoons corn syrup
1 cup yellow cornmeal
2 cups cooking oil

1

Mix egg, honey and syrup together. Then dip fillet in batter and roll in yellow cornmeal.

2

Heat cooking oil in Dutch oven as hot as possible. Drop fish in oil. It will sink to bottom and then rise back to the top when done. (Mr. Haggard suggests you use gas flame to obtain heat needed to boil grease.)

Yield: four servings.

Janos Starker

Hungarian-born cellist Janos Starker brings this dish to us from
his homeland.

FISH PAPRIKAS

5 pounds fish (carp, whitefish,
perch)
2 tablespoons salt

4 large onions, finely chopped
fish stock
3 tablespoons paprika
2 green peppers, coarsely chopped

1

Cut fish into two-inch strips. Sprinkle with salt and let stand one hour.

2

In bottom of a large casserole which can be used on top of stove, sprinkle
one-third of the chopped onions, then a layer of fish. Continue layering
ending with onion.

3

Pour on enough fish stock to cover two-thirds of the fish and onions.
Bring to a boil. Add paprika and green peppers. Cook until fish flakes.
Season to taste, then let stand ten minutes before serving.

4

To serve cold arrange cooked fish in individual serving dishes.
Pour on fish stock, chill until jellied.
Yield: eight servings.

Fish Stock:
1 pound fish heads
1 large onion, chopped
1 tablespoon salt

3 stalks celery, chopped
2 carrots, chopped
water to cover

1

Combine first five ingredients. Add water to cover; simmer one hour,
then strain.

Antal Dorati

Founding Artist Antal Dorati who brought this recipe from his native Hungary is a renowned conductor who is now the Music Director and Conductor of the National Symphony.

COLD FOGAS

2 pounds fresh fish (flounder, sole etc., one-half pound per person)
2 cups water

2 tablespoons vinegar
½ teaspoon salt
1 large onion, sliced
cheesecloth

Salad ingredients:
½ cup potatoes, cooked and diced
½ cup beets, cooked and diced
½ cup carrots, cooked and diced
½ cup peas, cooked
1 apple, cored and sliced

1 can herrings, cut into bite-size pieces
¾ cup mayonnaise
2 tablespoons unflavored gelatin
¾ cup cold water
smoked salmon as garnish

Day before serving
1
Make marinating sauce by combining water, vinegar, salt and onion. Bring to a boil and cool to lukewarm.
2
Clean fish and remove center bones.
3
Tie fish in cheesecloth and poach in marinade until tender. Let fish cool in sauce. Then chill.

Day of serving
1
Carefully remove skin from fish and cut fish into even slices.
2
Combine salad ingredients with one half cup mayonnaise and arrange as a mound on large serving plate.
3
Dissolve gelatin in water. While it is still liquid, paint fish slices two or three times to make shiny.
4
Place slices of fish on top of salad arranged like a wreath. Use decorator's tube to garnish fish with thick mayonnaise. Decorate with slices of smoked salmon twisted into curls.
Yield: four servings.

Diahann Carroll

Kennedy Center Founding Artist Diahann Carroll is a famous singer as well as television star and sang to a standing ovation when she gave a concert here in the Fall of 1972.

FRESH FISH AND VEGETABLE POTPOURRI

4 fresh trout
4 fresh halibut
2 bunches of fresh spinach
2 cups pea pods
2 cups bean sprouts
2 cups water chestnuts
½ cup safflower oil

dry mustard
salt
pepper
Lawry's seasoning salt
Worcestershire sauce
soy sauce
(use seasonings according to taste)

1
Marinate fish in soy sauce, Worcestershire sauce, Lawry's seasoning salt, pepper and salt for one hour.
2
Cover bottom of large copper (if available) skillet with enough safflower oil to keep pan moist.
3
Place one layer of all vegetables in pan. Sprinkle a dash of dry mustard over vegetables and start cooking over low flame.
4
Place halibut on bed of vegetables, add another layer of vegetables, repeat dash of dry mustard, place trout on second layer of vegetables.
5
Cover and steam for 25 to 30 minutes.
Yield: eight servings.

Ingrid Bergman

Miss Bergman, a living legend for thirty years, has starred in several dozen films and has won two Academy Awards (for "Gaslight" and "Anastasia"). When she performed at the Kennedy Center in "Captain Brassbound's Conversion" in March of 1972, the critics found her "irresistible."

"MR. JANSSON'S TEMPTATION"*
(A fish and potato casserole)

1 four-ounce can herrings
(preferably in dill sauce)
1 can anchovy fillets (about
twenty fillets)
8 medium potatoes (raw, peeled)
3 to 4 onions (very thinly sliced)

½ stick butter
3 to 4 tablespoons brine from
herring can
1 cup or more milk (cream if you
prefer)

1
Butter a two-quart baking dish and preheat oven to 450 degrees.
2
Put slices of raw, peeled potatoes ("I make them stand up"), raw slices of onions and the herrings alternately in rows until casserole is filled.
3
Put dabs of butter here and there, add the milk and brine from the herring can ("not too much, it might get too salty"). Place anchovies on top.
4
Bake until potatoes are soft, 45 minutes to one hour.
5
Serve hot from the dish with ice cold aquavit and beer and hard rye bread.
Yield: four to six servings.

*Mr. Jansson, a Swedish preacher of a century ago, was caught by his parishoners indulging in this dish after he had publicly professed to be fasting.

Percy Heath

Founding Artist Percy Heath, a member of the Modern Jazz Quartet, explains about his recipe: "A fishing lady friend of ours gave us this method of frying striped bass, which she calls Uncle Buddies. Both our families vacation at Montauk Point, where we chase the 'Striper' night and day, so we have freshly caught bass on hand all summer."

UNCLE BUDDIES

1 bass fillet
½ cup white vinegar
½ cup pancake flour

2 cups peanut oil
1 lemon

1
Skin fillet, cut into three-inch pieces, dip into white vinegar, then pancake flour and deep fry in oil.
2
Serve with lemon wedges
"Yum, Yum," writes Mr. Heath
Yield: two servings.

Kenneth Klein

Kenneth Klein is the Conductor and Music Director of the Guadalajara Symphony in Guadalajara, Mexico.

TROUT WITH WINE AND MINT SAUCE

8 trout (about one pound each)
flour
salt
pepper
4 tablespoons butter

4 tablespoons olive oil
2 cups dry white wine
2 tablespoons fresh mint, chopped
juice of one lemon
juice of one lime

1
Season trout with salt and pepper and dust lightly with flour. Brown in butter and oil, no longer than five minutes on each side.

2
Remove fish to hot platter and to the pan liquids add the wine, mint, lemon, and lime juice and simmer for about eight minutes.

3
Pour over fish and serve garnished with fresh sprigs of mint.
Yield: eight servings.

Poultry

POULTRY

Sergiu Luca

Sergiu Luca plays the violin and especially likes to play with the Lincoln Center Chamber Music Quartet. He says the recipe below is called the "Chamber Music Chicken Wings" because "it seems to be our favorite post chamber music snack. The first time we played quartets, I prepared four pounds of it for four people but that was not enough. The next time I tried eight pounds for a viola quintet session and we still ran out. I have therefore now standardized the recipe to six pounds for four people but I wouldn't guarantee that it will hold out."

"CHAMBER MUSIC CHICKEN WINGS"

6 pounds chicken wings
  vegetable oil for deep frying
2 tablespoons rice vinegar
2 tablespoons fresh ginger root,
  finely chopped
½ teaspoon garlic powder
6 tablespoons soy sauce

2 tablespoons Mirin (Japanese sweet
  cooking wine)
5 tablespoons sugar
2 teaspoons "Five Spice"
  (obtainable in a Chinese grocery)
1 tablespoon lemon juice

1
Cut chicken wings at the joint. In a wok or deep skillet heat oil until smoking.
Deep fry chicken wings until golden brown. Drain chicken wings on
paper towels.
2
Place remaining ingredients in wok and blend over low heat. Turn heat off,
add chicken wings and let them marinate for several hours.
Turn occasionally to insure a thorough mixing.
3
Just before serving (which can be as much as twenty-four hours later,
if wings and marinade are kept in refrigerator covered) put over moderately
high heat and stir chicken wings until marinade is reduced and coats
the chicken wings.
Yield: four servings.

Fifth Dimension

Founding Artist Ron Townson is a member of "The Fifth Dimension," the famous popular singing group.

CHERRY CHICKEN SURPRISE

1 three pound chicken, cut up
  into pieces
1 large can black, pitless, bing
  cherries
2 tablespoons sugar
salt

pepper
garlic salt
paprika
cashew nuts
parsley
½ cup vegetable oil

1
Brown chicken in oil then season to taste with salt, pepper, garlic salt and paprika.

2
In a separate sauce pan, pour can of cherries with juice, add sugar and stir until thickened.

3
Put chicken into shallow baking pan, put into 350 degree oven and bake until done, about one hour.

4
When chicken is done, pour thickened cherries and juice over it, garnish with nuts and parsley and serve.

Yield: four servings.

POULTRY

Gina Bachauer

Founding Artist and concert pianist Gina Bachauer writes the following about her recipe: "Some years ago, during one of my concert tours in the United States, the President of the Symphony Orchestra in a certain city invited me to stay at his home. He and his wife were charming, informal people and one day I offered to cook chicken with almonds for them . . . The meal was a great success but I had cooked far too generously and even after second helpings all round, a good deal was left over. The following year I was again performing with the Symphony Orchestra in that city and once more stayed at the President's home. When I arrived, my hostess greeted me very warmly and with a big smile told me she had a surprise for me that evening. When we sat down to dinner, the maid brought in a dish of chicken with almonds. 'Ah!' , I exclaimed, 'I see you have learned to cook my favorite dish.' 'Oh, no' said my hostess, 'Your dish last year was so wonderful I kept the leftovers in the deep freeze for a special occasion—your return this year!'
"Note: I do NOT recommend keeping this dish in a freezer for one year!"

CHICKEN WITH ALMONDS

2 roasting chickens
½ pound roasted ground almonds
½ pound butter
1 cup olive oil
½ cup dry white wine
½ cup dry red wine

½ cup Sherry
2 tablespoons corn starch
salt
pepper
paprika

1

Quarter chickens and brown them with the olive oil. When well-browned, place chickens and oil in a casserole with the butter and three wines. Salt and pepper to taste and add a dash of paprika. Cook over slow fire, covered, for two hours.

2

When ready, cut chicken into medium sized pieces, remove all bones and put in serving dish and keep hot.

3

Pour gravy into cooking pan, add cornstarch (diluted in half a cup lukewarm water) and stir continuously over low flame until the sauce becomes thick.

4

Cover chicken with this sauce, sprinkle hot roasted almonds on top and serve.
Yield: eight servings.

Mimi Paul

Mimi Paul has been a principal ballet dancer with the American Ballet Theatre. She says the dish below combines tasty with economical.

CHICKEN BREASTS PIQUANT

4 whole chicken breasts, halved
1½ cups dry red wine
½ cup soy sauce
½ cup salad oil
4 tablespoons water

2 cloves garlic, sliced
2 teaspoons ground ginger
½ teaspoon oregano
2 tablespoons brown sugar

1
Arrange chicken breasts in baking dish.
2
Mix all other ingredients and pour over chicken breasts.
3
Preheat oven to 375 degrees then bake for about one hour. If desired chicken dish can be refrigerated or frozen. When ready to eat return to room temperature, then bake.
Yield: six to eight servings.

POULTRY

Dame Margot Fonteyn

Dame Margot Fonteyn, ballet's prima ballerina, has appeared as a guest performer several times with the National Ballet. The recipe below was sent by Dame Margot's sister-in-law at the dancer's request because, she explained, her adventures in the kitchen are limited to grilling a steak!

CHICKEN BREASTS WITH SOUR CREAM AND BRANDY

2 chicken breasts
½ cup unsalted butter
½ cup sour cream
1 chicken bouillon cube
2 tablespoons brandy
1 tablespoon flour

salt
pepper
pinch of sweet basil
pinch of tarragon
¼ cup boiling water

1

Melt the butter in a skillet and gently saute the chicken until it is cooked through (about fifteen minutes). Remove chicken from the pan and keep warm in a serving dish.

2

Add flour to the butter left in the pan, mix to a roux and cook gently for two to three minutes. Make chicken stock with bouillon cube and one fourth cup water, add to the pan and mix to a thick sauce. Add salt, pepper and herbs, seasoning to taste.

3

Add brandy and mix, then add sour cream and mix well, and heat to a cream consistency. Adjust seasoning. Pour over chicken in serving dish, decorate with sprigs of parsley, and it is ready to serve.

Yield: two servings.

Julius Rudel

Mr. Rudel, a great friend of the Center, is a Founding Artist as well as the Center's Music Director.

CHICKEN WITH CRUMBS

1 three-pound fryer, cut into small pieces
2 tablespoons melted margarine
1 clove garlic, crushed
2 sprigs parsley, minced

1 teaspoon dried rosemary, crushed
salt
pepper
1 cup corn flake crumbs

1
Wash chicken and dry on paper towels. Preheat oven to 375 degrees.

2
Place chicken flat in a baking pan, skin side up and sprinkle evenly with salt, pepper and rub with garlic, then sprinkle with parsley and rosemary.

3
Pour melted margarine evenly over chicken and then cover with corn flake crumbs.

4
Place in center of oven and bake for one hour to an hour and a half until crust is brown. (Chicken does not have to be turned or basted.)

Yield: four generous servings.

POULTRY

Hal Holbrook

Mr. Holbrook is an actor who has played many roles with great success. Perhaps his most famous role was his interpretation of Mark Twain which he created himself. He appeared at the Kennedy Center in Arthur Miller's "The Creation of the World and other Business." About chicken livers, he says, "When I was a boy in Ohio and New England I wouldn't eat a chicken liver for anything, but this is what sophistication has done for me. Plus my wife's cooking."

CHICKEN LIVERS HOLBROOK

1 pound chicken livers
½ stick butter or margarine
3 or 4 scallions, cut in small pieces
2 tablespoons (at least) Worcestershire sauce

½ cup dry white wine (at least)
fines herbs
salt
pepper

1

Saute the chicken livers and scallions in the butter, Worcestershire sauce and white wine. "Use serious amounts of both; don't drown them but we are trying to create a decent amount of sauce. Sprinkle fearlessly with fines herbs, a small amount of salt and ground pepper if you like.

2

"All this would be accomplished on a low heat gently turning with wooden spoon. Should take 6 to 12 minutes depending on the relative doneness of chicken livers. I personally am a fan of doneness."

Serve with rice, and endive and watercress salad.

Yield: two generous servings.

(signature)

The great and venerable conductor of the Philadelphia Orchestra made his appearance to unanimous acclaim soon after the Center opened.

CHICKEN IN SHERRY WINE

1 three-pound chicken, cut into pieces
4 tablespoons flour
4 teaspoons paprika
salt

pepper
1 stick butter
¾ cup chicken stock
⅓ cup good dry sherry
½ cup heavy cream

1
Wash and dry chicken. Dip pieces into mixture of flour, paprika, salt and pepper.

2
Brown quickly in butter and place in heavy casserole (or keep in deep skillet).

3
Pour chicken stock and sherry over chicken, cover tightly and simmer gently for one hour.

4
When chicken is cooked remove to heated platter and keep hot. Add cream and scant teaspoon of leftover flour-paprika mixture. Stir until sauce thickens without letting it boil. Pour over chicken and serve.

Yield: four servings.

Fernando Bujones

Mr. Bujones is a young principal in the American Ballet Theatre.

CUBAN CHICKEN FRICASSEE

2 three-pound chickens, cut into serving pieces
5 cloves garlic, finely chopped
1 onion, chopped
½ green pepper, chopped
2 large (fifteen ounce) cans tomato sauce
4 bay leaves

1 teaspoon cumin seed
1½ teaspoons dried leaf oregano
1 cup raisins
1 cup pimiento-stuffed olives
2 tablespoons corn oil
1 teaspoon vinegar
salt
pepper

1
Place chickens in heavy skillet or Dutch oven on top of stove.
Add remaining ingredients, cover and bring to a boil.
2
Reduce heat and simmer one hour, turning chicken occasionally.
3
Remove chicken to platter, serve sauce over rice.
Yield: six to eight servings.

Elaine Joyce

Singer-actress Elaine Joyce played the female lead in "Sugar" a musical adaptation of the play, "Some Like it Hot." She writes about her recipe: "This is Hungarian-style chicken handed down to me from my mother. They say the best way to start this dish is to first go out and steal a chicken."

HUNGARIAN CREAMED CHICKEN

1 three-pound chicken, cut into pieces
2 tablespoons cooking oil
½ onion, chopped
1 teaspoon paprika

½ pint sour cream
2 tablespoons flour
1 cup water
salt
pepper

1
Brown chicken in oil until golden. Reduce heat, add salt, pepper, onion, paprika and one-half cup water; cover and continue cooking for an hour.

2
Remove chicken to warm platter, then add sour cream and flour mixed with remaining water to liquid, bring to boil, correct seasonings, pour over chicken and serve.
Yield: four servings.

Mr. Stevenson, the National Ballet's Director (with Frederic Franklin)
offers this interesting chicken dish which he says he first tasted
in Chile, but originates in Mexico.

POLLO MOLE

1 large chicken, cut into pieces
salt
2 bay leaves
water
4 tablespoons olive oil
2 cloves garlic
1 medium onion, chopped
1 green pepper, chopped
2 large tomatoes, coarsely
chopped
3 slices canned pimentos
2 tablespoons chili powder
2½ cups chicken stock

½ cup ground almonds
½ cup ground peanuts
½ teaspoon anise seeds
¼ cup seeded raisins
1 orange rind, grated
⅛ teaspoon powdered cinnamon
2 pinches nutmeg
2 pinches powdered cloves
black pepper
dash of Tabasco
2 squares bitter chocolate
½ cup light rum

1
Place the pieces of chicken in pot with bay leaves and enough salted
water to cook. When almost tender remove chicken and drain through
colander. Reserve stock.

2
Put olive oil in heavy skillet with garlic. When oil is hot, brown chicken,
remove and drain.

3
To oil add onion, pepper, tomatoes and pimentos. When vegetables are
tender, add chili powder and blend. Then add chicken stock, nuts and
anise, raisins, orange rind, cinnamon, nutmeg, cloves, pepper and Tabasco.
Simmer thirty minutes, stirring often.

4
Put chicken in sauce and shave chocolate over the top. Cover and simmer
thirty minutes more. Five minutes before serving, add rum.
Yield: six servings.

Marilyn

Founding Artist and singer Marilyn McCoo is a member of the famed "The Fifth Dimension," one of the most popular singing groups in the country.

"POULET COCOTTE A LA McCOO"

8 to 12 pieces of chicken (skinned if you prefer)
4 tablespoons vegetable oil
4 tablespoons parsley, chopped
3 stalks green onions, chopped
¾ cup Marsala wine
¼ cup water

2 cups fresh mushrooms
2 tablespoons butter
1 tablespoon lemon juice
rosemary
salt
pepper

1
Season chicken with salt and pepper and brown in vegetable oil over medium high flame.

2
Remove chicken and turn down flame, add parsley and green onions and saute for five minutes. Then add Marsala wine, water and rosemary to taste.

3
Put chicken back in skillet, cover and cook slowly thirty to forty minutes.

4
Ten minutes before chicken is done, saute mushrooms in butter, add to chicken mixture, pour lemon juice over all and serve.
Yield: four servings.

Earl Hines (signature)

Earl Hines who brought a unique, melodic style to jazz piano in the 1920's was still going strong at the Kennedy Center when he gave a Founding Artist performance in February of 1972. He describes his recipe below as "one that I never seem to tire of."

SMOTHERED CHICKEN AND STRING BEAN DINNER

1 medium-sized frying chicken (cut into pieces)
1 cup flour
2 tablespoons cooking oil
2½ tablespoons butter
1½ cups water
½ cup onions
2 pounds fresh green beans
2 ham-hocks
6 cups water
salt
pepper

1
Wash chicken and blot on paper towel. Salt and pepper to taste and lightly flour on all sides.

2
Barely cover a heavy skillet with cooking oil and add two and a half tablespoons of butter. Add chicken parts and brown over medium high heat. Add one cup of water after browning, cover and simmer over low heat for approximately thirty minutes or until well done.

3
Add one-half cup water and one half cup chopped onions. Cover and simmer slowly for approximately twenty minutes.

Beans
1
Select fresh green beans that are bright and clear in color (beans must snap when broken).

2
Add ham-hocks (pork bones) to six cups of water and let them boil until well done, at least an hour. The meat will fall apart when pierced with a fork.

3
Add green beans to ham-hocks and broth, salt and pepper to taste. Boil beans to tenderness and serve with smothered chicken.

Yield: four servings.

Eugenia Rawls

Eugenia Rawls starred in Jean Giradoux's play "The Enchanted" when it played at the Center. She says that Tallulah Bankhead loved the recipe below and always asked for it when she came for dinner.

TALLULAH'S CHICKEN

6 whole chicken breasts, halved
2 tablespoons butter
1 onion
1 apple, peeled

1 cup cream of mushroom soup
1 pint light cream
curry powder to taste
seedless grapes

1
Wash and pat dry split chicken breasts and arrange flat in buttered pyrex dish. Preheat oven to 350 degrees.

2
Slice onion and apple very thinly and saute in one tablespoon butter in frying pan.

3
Add soup and cream and curry powder. Stir all together over low heat and pour over chicken.

4
Bake, uncovered, basting occasionally in moderate oven until most of sauce is absorbed—about an hour and a half—and chicken is golden crusty.

5
Serve on platter garnished with seedless grapes.
Yield: six servings.

POULTRY

Founding Artist Victor Borge brought his great musical talent, his humor and his spontaneity to the Kennedy Center and his humor is evident even when he cooks.

ROCK CORNISH HENS

6 Rock Cornish pullets	1 tablespoon water (or more
¼ pound butter	to make paste)
1¼ cups water	3 teaspoons flour
salt	½ cup light cream
pepper	½ teaspoon sugar

1
Rub the insides of the pullets with salt and pepper.

2
Sear in butter in Dutch oven until golden brown—ten to twelve minutes. "If a clock is not available, all you've got to do is play the "Minute Waltz" ten to twelve times," says Mr. Borge.

3
Add water and let simmer, covered, until tender—approximately 35 minutes. "Here, the 'Dance of the Hour,' played half through will come in handy, if dragged slightly."

4
Remove birds.

To Prepare Sauce:

5
"Stir like crazy into drippings, a paste of cold water and three teaspoons flour."

6
Add one half cup light cream, salt, tasteless sauce coloring, and one half teaspoon sugar.

Pour sauce over pullets and serve

Yield: six servings.

Ham and Pork

Paul Callaway

Paul Callaway, an established organist, writes that the recipe below was taken from an out-of-print book called *Why Cook* "which is a big help to idiot cooks like myself."

BEER-GLAZED HAM

3 pound canned, boiled ham
1 teaspoon ground cloves
½ cup brown sugar

2 tablespoons mild prepared
  mustard
1 can beer

1

Place ham, fat side up, in a shallow baking pan. Use a rack or make small balls of aluminum wrap to lift the ham about one-fourth inch from the pan. Preheat oven to 325 degrees.

2

Mix cloves, brown sugar and mustard and spread over ham.

3

Pour beer into pan and place in oven and bake for about an hour basting every ten minutes.

Yield: six servings.

John Alexander

Metropolitan Opera tenor John Alexander has given us this delicious fruited ham recipe.

FRUITED HAM WITH COGNAC

1 boneless precooked ham, 5 to 6 pounds
½ cup honey (cranberry-flavored if possible)
½ cup pineapple wedges (fresh or canned)

12 maraschino cherries
6 tablespoons maraschino cherry liquid
whole cloves (those from Tanzania are the most aromatic)
½ cup cognac

1

Preheat oven to 325 degrees. If you use a canned ham, remove gelatin that may cling to it, then score the fatty side of the ham and place a whole clove in the center of each diamond.

2

Blend honey, pineapple (which has been drained), cherries and cherry juice in an electric blender at high speed, or mash all together until it makes thick pulp.

3

Pour honey mixture over the ham, coating as evenly as possible.

4

Bake half an hour, but check after fifteen minutes. If there is any excess of fatty liquid in the baking pan, be sure to drain it off. The ham must be thickly glazed when finished, and too much liquid retards the glazing.

5

After half an hour begin basting with cognac, letting it combine with some of the honey mixture in the pan. Do this for thirty minutes until the ham has turned a rich cherry red and the glaze has thickened. If you like, the ham can be decorated before baking with thin slices of pineapple and some of the cherries cut in half.

Yield: ten to twelve servings.

Walter Susskind

Walter Susskind, Music Director and Conductor of the St. Louis Symphony, has appeared several times at the Center. He says that in his native Czechoslovakia, pork usually is served as roast with dumplings and sauerkraut, but he prefers it as it is in his recipe below.

APRICOT-RAISIN PORK CHOPS

6 pork chops, one-inch thick with pockets
2 tablespoons cooking oil
1 cup flour
½ teaspoon salt
⅛ teaspoon pepper
⅛ teaspoon paprika

½ teaspoon oregano
1 seventeen-ounce can apricot halves
1 cup golden raisins
1½ tablespoons caraway seeds
1 cup water
½ cup brown sugar

1
Brown chops on both sides in cooking oil over medium heat. Remove chops from skillet and place two apricot halves in pocket of each chop. Rub mixture of flour, salt, pepper, paprika and oregano over chops. Return to skillet and brown again on both sides.

2
Cut up remaining apricots and combine with raisins, caraway seeds, apricot syrup, water, and brown sugar. Preheat oven to 350 degrees.

3
Put chops in casserole, pour sauce over chops and bake covered in 350° oven for forty-five minutes. Uncover and bake fifteen minutes longer. Serve over saffron rice.
Yield: six servings.

MILOS FORMAN

Mr. Forman is an award-winning film director. "The Little Black Book," which he directed at the Kennedy Center was his first attempt at stage direction.

CHINESE PORK WITH SPINACH

1 pound pork rump roast, sliced into thin strips
2 eggs
1 teaspoon corn or potato starch
3 tablespoons vegetable oil
2 teaspoons bacon fat
1 teaspoon monosodium glutamate
1 cup beef broth

1 tablespoon soy sauce
2 tablespoons white wine
1 package frozen spinach, cooked
1 handful black Chinese mushrooms (if handy)
1 teaspoon hot red peppers, crushed
pinch of black pepper
pinch of salt

1
Soak meat in combination of salt, eggs and corn starch for minimum of ten minutes.

2
Then quickly brown meat in two tablespoons of vegetable oil, then drain on paper towel.

3
Melt bacon fat over medium heat in frying pan and add monosodium glutamate, beef broth, soy sauce and wine, spinach and mushrooms and cover for two minutes to steam.

4
Meanwhile heat one tablespoon vegetable oil in a small frying pan. When hot add crushed red peppers and ground black pepper for three or four seconds. Then pour this mixture into pork mixture.
Serve immediately with rice.
Yield: four servings.

Gordon Davidson

Gordon Davidson, who directed the Kennedy Center production of "Mass" writes that on the subject of cooking he and his wife work as a team (he does the eating and she does the cooking). The Davidson "team" sent the recipe below describing it as a favorite family dish.

PORK CHOP CASSEROLE

4 or 8 pork chops (depending on size)
1 can cream of mushroom soup (or Cheddar cheese soup)

1 cup whole milk
salt
pepper

1
Brown pork chops in skillet, then place in casserole. Season with salt and pepper. Mix soup and milk together and pour over the chops.

2
Bake, covered, at 325 degrees for half an hour. Remove cover and cook until done, about fifteen minutes more. Serve with rice or noodles and a salad.

Yield: four servings.

Roberta Peters

Miss Peters, the famous opera soprano, writes about her recipe: "I call this recipe 'Opera Spareribs' because I have prepared it from time to time for groups of my opera colleagues. My experience with them has been that they are all hearty eaters either by reason of their calling or possibly because they like what they are eating. In any event (if you will pardon the pun) don't spare the ribs."

"OPERA SPARERIBS"

5 pounds spareribs
   salt
   pepper
   rosemary

1 cup honey
1 can concentrated orange juice
¼ cup lemon juice

1

Clean and cut spareribs into sections. Rub salt, pepper and rosemary (to taste) over ribs.

2

Broil slowly either in a rotisserie or on a barbecue until half done. Add combination of honey, orange juice and lemon juice to ribs on both sides and continue cooking until crisp and brown.

Yield: five servings.

Veal

VEAL

Dorothy Kirsten, the famous Metropolitan Opera star, says of the recipe below, "I first learned to prepare veal in this way when I was a student in Italy. The simplicity of this dish immediately appealed to me and it has been one of the regulars in my kitchen ever since."

OSSO BUCO
(Italian veal Stew)

2 or 3 pounds knuckle of veal	sprig of thyme
3 or 4 carrots	1 bay leaf
1 or 2 stalks celery	1 tablespoon flour
1 cup white wine, veal stock or water	1 tablespoon butter
1 cup tomato pulp	salt
strip of lemon peel	pepper

1

Have the butcher saw the veal in two-inch lengths, not chopped, as the marrow must remain inside the bone.

2

Chop the vegetables very fine and place them in saucepan and saute them in butter. Add the meat and season highly with salt and pepper.

3

When vegetables and meat are well browned add tablespoon of flour mixed with a little water. Add the tomato pulp, the wine and sufficient stock or water to barely cover the meat. Add the herbs, tied together.

4

Simmer gently for one and one half to two hours. Ten minutes before serving take the meat from the saucepan and strain the sauce, removing the herb bouquet. Place meat and strained sauce on platter, sprinkle with lemon peel and parsley and serve.

Yield: four servings.

Zoe Caldwell

The Australian born Zoe Caldwell is famed for her roles as the school marm in "The Prime of Miss Jean Brodie," Cleopatra, Colette, Ophelia, "Saint Joan" and she brought her special style to the role of Eve in "The Creation of the World and Other Business" which played in Washington in the late fall of 1972.

ROAST LOIN OF VEAL

1 five-pound loin of veal
1 to one and one half sticks butter, softened
1 eight ounce jar Dijon mustard

1½ cups chicken broth
salt
pepper

1
Salt and pepper the loin of veal. Preheat oven to 325°.
2
Mix together equal parts of butter and Dijon mustard until thoroughly blended. Spread half of this mixture over the loin of veal periodically basting.
3
When veal is half-cooked, take it out of the oven and spread the rest of the butter-mustard mixture over it. Return to oven and continue to baste.
4
When veal is cooked (allow twenty five to thirty minutes per pound), remove from roasting pan. Add hot chicken broth to pan juices and pour all over the veal and serve.

Note: I vary putting the veal on a bed of buttered noodles or on mashed parsnips.
Yield: Six servings.

Beverly Sills

Beverly Sills is one of the most acclaimed opera sopranos of our time. She writes briefly about cooking "As a cooker, I prefer to sing."

VEAL PARMIGIANA

1 cup bread crumbs (seasoned)
½ cup fresh Parmesan cheese, grated
1 small can tomato paste
¾ cup good dry red wine
1 stick butter

4 tablespoons olive oil
12 small, very thin slices of veal
2 beaten eggs mixed with a little water
12 thin slices Mozzarella cheese

1
Mix Parmesan cheese and crumbs well. Combine tomato paste and red wine.

2
Melt butter and oil in large skillet. Dip veal slices first in beaten eggs, then crumb-cheese mixture and fry quickly, about three minutes on each side. Preheat oven to 350°.

3
Place four slices of the cooked veal in the bottom of a large baking dish, cover with four slices of Mozzarella, then with one third tomato-wine sauce. Repeat two more times, then shake Parmesan cheese over the top and bake for fifteen minutes.

Note: If it begins to dry out, add a little dry vermouth.

Yield: four servings.

Beef

Eugene Istomin

Mr. Istomin is a grand master of the piano and recognized as a brilliant interpreter of nineteenth-century music.

BEEFSTEAK WORONOFF

4 one-half pound slices of filet of beef
½ pound butter
½ teaspoon rosemary (if you prefer—use tarragon)
salt

pepper

Sauce:
⅓ teaspoon Dijon mustard
2 teaspoons Worcestershire sauce
5 tablespoons cognac

1
Combine ingredients for the sauce, mixing thoroughly.

2
Heat half the butter in the skillet and add beef slices and rosemary. Cook very quickly over high heat. Two minutes for each side is sufficient.

3
Season to taste, add balance of the butter and the sauce, continue cooking for two minutes more, no longer.

4
Turn the meat once during the cooking and serve with sauce slightly reduced and strained.

Yield: four servings.

Frederic Franklin

Mr. Franklin is a director of the National Ballet whose home is here in Washington. About his recipe he says "It is partly my own concoction and being English and brought up on curry, it is a special favorite. I have served it to many of the dancers—it isn't fattening (omit the bread); they all enjoyed it."

BEEF CURRY

2 pounds flank steak
½ cup flour
10 small white onions, peeled
6 carrots, peeled and cut into
   julienne strips
2 green peppers, seeded and
   quartered
2 teaspoons tomato paste

2 cans beef bouillon
½ teaspoon oregano
1 tablespoon curry powder—or
   more to taste
1 clove garlic, mashed
2 tablespoons butter
1 tablespoon oil

1

Cut meat into one-inch cubes and dredge in flour. Heat butter and oil in skillet and brown on all sides. Remove to large ovenproof casserole. Preheat oven to 325°.

2

Add curry powder to skillet (more butter if necessary), and cook three minutes, stirring constantly. Then add one and one half cans beef bouillon and scrape bottom of skillet for brown particles of meat. Add tomato paste, stirring until mixture begins to thicken. Add garlic and oregano and simmer for three minutes.

3

Cover meat in casserole with soup mixture and simmer on top of stove for one half hour.

4

Add vegetables and pour remaining bouillon over all. Place covered casserole in oven for one and one half hours. Meat is ready when it can be easily pierced with a fork.

Serve with good chutney, red wine and hot French bread.

Yield: four to six servings.

BEEF

Sally Rand

Miss Rand gained instant fame when she first performed her "Fan Dance" many years ago and she has stayed famous because of her ability to entertain. About her recipe she says "When I'm affluent I use Filet Mignon. Less choice cuts of beef should be tenderized with meat tenderizer."

MY BEEF STEW

2 pounds good quality chuck, cut in one inch cubes
1 large can tiny new potatoes. "I use canned ones, hate to peel new ones," writes Miss Rand.
1 large can tiny, white onions

½ cup good dry sherry
½ cup flour
1 tablespoon garlic salt
pepper to taste
pinch of dehydrated garlic flakes
3 tablespoons cooking oil

1
Dampen meat with a little water or sherry; season with salt and pepper and dredge with flour.

2
Heat oil to almost smoking in skillet and quickly brown meat. Remove meat to heavy Dutch oven, add water to cover . Add garlic flakes and continue cooking.

3
Pour grease from frying pan (leave scrapings); add potatoes and onions with liquid and pour all into Dutch oven. Simmer until liquid is reduced to thick gravy.

4
Add one-half cup sherry and simmer until ready to serve. "Don't cook too long; potatoes and onions get mushy from the moment you add water to the meat, stir frequently to keep from sticking. Serve in a big tureen with a dipper, or cup. This stew is to be eaten from wide soup bowls, not plates" writes Miss Rand.
Yield: four servings.

BEEF

Alexander Schneider (signature)

Mr. Schneider, conductor and violinist, conducted part of the May 1973 Bach Festival held at the Center. He says that the recipe below is one of his favorites "but I warn you, it is a heavy dish and one must have lots of good wine. I suggest a very good Beaujolais or if you have more money, a beautiful Bordeaux-'64 or '66."

BLOOD SAUSAGE AND BRAINS

4 tablespoons cooking oil
1 stick butter
8 French blood sausages
8 calves brains

6 scallions, chopped
salt
pepper

1
Put two tablespoons oil in each pan and when hot,
melt one half stick of butter in each pan.

2
Put sausages in one pan, brains in the other, add chopped scallions
to sausage pan and salt and pepper to both.

3
Fry slowly, stirring, no more than ten minutes. Sausages will break apart.
Cut into brains, if there is no sign of blood they are done. Mix together.
Yield: eight servings.

Mr. Schneider serves the sausage and brains dish with a potato salad recipe which appears in our section on potatoes and vegetables. He adds "I usually serve this with a green salad on the side, but my salad is very special and I can't give it to you now. Perhaps I'll give it to you another time—in 20 years."

Misha Dichter

Pianist Misha Dichter loves this recipe which his Brazilian-born wife, Cipa, taught him.

BRAZILIAN BEANS AND RICE

Beans:
4 cups water
1 pound black beans
1 pound lean beef (sausage, chicken livers, pigs feet may be added)
4 ripe tomatoes, chopped

2 cloves garlic, minced
2 medium onions, chopped
2 tablespoons cooking oil
4 sprigs parsley, minced
salt
pepper
pinch of sugar

1
Wash beans thoroughly, then soak overnight in water.

2
Add meat without discarding water in which beans have been soaked. Bring to a boil, reduce heat, cover and continue cooking until beans are tender (about two hours).

3
Heat oil in frying pan and saute onions, garlic and parsley. When onions are transparent, add tomatoes, season with salt, pepper and sugar and cook ten minutes longer.

4
Blend three heaping tablespoons of cooked beans into tomato sauce and saute for a few minutes. Stir this mixture into the pot and let simmer with beans and meat for fifteen minutes, then serve with rice (recipe below).

Rice:
2 tablespoons cooking oil
1 small onion, chopped
2 cloves garlic, minced

2 bay leaves
2 cups uncooked rice
4 cups salted boiling water

1
In a heavy pot, heat oil and saute onion, garlic and bay leaves, stirring with a wooden spoon to prevent burning.

2
Blend in rice and continue cooking until rice is cooked and golden looking. Add boiling water, one cupful at a time, cover and simmer over low heat until water is absorbed and rice is tender.
Yield: six servings.

Jack Lowe & Arthur Whittemore

Acknowledged as music's foremost duo-pianists, Mr. Whittemore and Mr. Lowe have been a professional team since they met in high school.

FRENCH BEEF AND VEGETABLE CASSEROLE

6 slices bacon	½ teaspoon thyme
2 pounds lean beef chuck, cut into cubes	1½ cups beef broth
½ cup flour	4 medium potatoes, peeled and quartered
1 teaspoon salt	12 small white onions, peeled
1 cup dry red wine	6 carrots, sliced lengthwise
2 tablespoons parsley	1 cup mushrooms, finely chopped
½ clove garlic	

1
Cook bacon until crisp; drain on paper towel and reserve drippings.
2
Dredge beef cubes in mixture of flour and salt. Then brown cubes in bacon drippings and remove to two-quart casserole.
3
Pour wine, parsley, garlic, thyme and beef broth into electric blender and blend until solid ingredients are pureed. Pour over meat in casserole.
4
Cover casserole; bake at 350 degrees for one hour. Stir potatoes, onions and carrots into casserole. Replace cover and bake additional hour or until vegetables are done. Stir in mushrooms (previously sauteed); scatter crumbled bacon on top with additional parsley as garnish.
Yield: four servings.

Stephen Schwartz

Stephen Schwartz, the composer and lyricist of "Godspell" and "Pippin," also co-authored the English text of "Mass" with Leonard Bernstein. His wife writes that the recipe below which is pronounced (gawumbki) has been in her family for generations.

GOLABKI
(Old Country Polish Stuffed Cabbage)

1 head cabbage	1 can sliced mushrooms
1 pound ground beef	3 pieces dried mushrooms
1 pound ground pork	(optional)
1 onion, minced	1 can tomato soup
1 onion, sliced	5 tablespoons butter
¾ cup rice	2 tablespoons flour
2 tablespoons soy sauce	salt
¼ cup milk	pepper

1
Remove core from whole head of cabbage. Place cabbage in large kettle of boiling water. Simmer until leaves are easily separated. Separate and allow to cool. Trim core off each leaf.

2
Cook rice according to directions on package.

3
Saute minced onion in butter until transparent. Then combine meat, rice, sauteed onion, milk and seasonings and mix well.

4
Place meat and rice mixture on cabbage leaf, fold in both sides of leaf and roll, starting with one of the open ends. Preheat oven to 325 degrees.

5
Place two tablespoons of butter and one-half sliced raw onion in roasting pan. Add remaining onion and any leftover cabbage leaves, as well as the rest of the butter on top. Over this add the tomato soup, dried mushrooms, and enough hot water to cover.

6
Roast at 325 degrees for one and one half hours. Then mix flour with one half cup water and add to thicken sauce. Roast an additional hour.

Yield: six to eight servings.

Arthur Fiedler

Boston Pops Orchestra Conductor Arthur Fiedler has appeared several times at the Center giving great pleasure to his audiences with his own inimitable style and talent.

ARTHUR FIEDLER'S GOULASH

2 pounds bottom round
1 large onion, chopped
1 clove garlic, chopped
3 tablespoons butter
¾ tablespoon paprika, or more
  if you prefer

salt
pepper
boiling water
1 tablespoon flour

1
Cut fat off meat and cube into medium-sized pieces.
2
Lightly brown onion and garlic with two tablespoons of the butter.
3
Melt remaining butter in large frying pan and brown meat on all sides, add browned onion and garlic to meat, and paprika, salt and pepper to taste. Mix ingredients well.
4
Start adding boiling water, keeping meat just covered with it for two or three hours or until meat is tender. Watch or check water during cooking time to make sure the meat is covered by enough "juice." Cook without a top on skillet.
5
When goulash is finished, add small amount of flour to juice to make it slightly thickened.
Yield: four servings.

BEEF

Ilse von Alpenheim

Ilse von Alpenheim is a concert pianist who also is married to the National Symphony's Music Director and Conductor.

HONG KONG RICE

2 cups rice
1 onion, finely chopped
½ pepperoni
7 ounces fillet of beef, cut into cubes
2 tablespoons cooking oil

3 eggs
2 tablespoons soy sauce
½ pound shrimp
juice of half a lemon
salt
pepper

1
Boil two cups of rice in the morning and leave to cool until evening.
2
Steam the onion, pepperoni and beef in the oil in a large pan.
3
Add the eggs which have been beaten with salt, pepper and soy sauce.
4
When the eggs begin to curdle, add the cold rice and shrimps sprinkled with lemon juice. Mix well and season with more soy sauce if desired.
Note: Jasmine tea is delicious with this dish.
Yield: four servings.

BEEF

Burt Bacharach

Artist Burt Bacharach appeared at the Kennedy Center in a concert
in the Fall of 1972 where he played the piano, sang and conducted
the orchestra for an evening of the incomparable music
which he composed.

MARINATED FLANK STEAK

1 two pound flank steak
1 tablespoon sugar
2 tablespoons dry sherry

2 tablespoons soy sauce
1 tablespoon honey

1
Marinate the steak in above ingredients all day, basting periodically.
2
Broil or grill on a barbecue.
Yield: four servings.

BEEF

Norman Scribner

Norman Scribner is the Music Director of the Choral Arts Society of Washington. The recipe below comes from a store of Syrian recipes handed down to Mrs. Scribner by her mother.

MUSHROOMS AND MEATBALLS

1 pound ground chuck
  salt to taste
  pepper to taste
  allspice to taste
2 tablespoons bread crumbs
  (approximately)

2 cups cooking oil
3 pounds mushrooms
½ glass water
1 cup rice

1

Mix ground meat with salt, pepper and allspice to taste. Add bread crumbs and a few drops of water as needed to make meat right consistency for forming tiny meatballs.

2

Fry meatballs in oil until brown, then dump out excess oil.

3

Clean mushrooms and drop into pot. Add one half glass water and season to taste. Cover and simmer for one and one half hours.

4

Cook the rice and pour meatball dish over it.

Yield: four servings.

Julie Harris

Miss Harris hypnotized her audience by her performance of the former Mary Todd in the production of "The Last of Mrs. Lincoln." She says she loves this recipe "because when I am working it is a complete meal and is better the second day than the first." We love the recipe in part because it was the first one we received from an artist.

POT ROAST WITH WINE AND OLIVES

1 five-pound pot roast (rump or bottom round)
12 whole pimento-stuffed olives
3 cloves garlic, sliced
1 medium onion, sliced
1 stalk celery, cut into one-inch pieces
1 bay leaf
4 whole cloves
1 tablespoon sugar
¼ tablespoon savory
1½ cups dry red wine
salt
pepper
4 potatoes, peeled and halved
4 carrots, peeled and diced
1 cup tomatoes, diced
½ cup pimento-stuffed olives, sliced

1
Cut deep slashes into fat side of roast, insert whole olive and slice of garlic into each slash. Add onion, celery, bay leaf, cloves, sugar, savory salt and pepper and sliced olives. Pour wine over all, cover and marinate in refrigerator overnight.

2
When ready to cook, heat about two tablespoons salad oil in large heavy skillet or Dutch oven and brown meat on all sides. Drain off fat. Add the marinade, cover tightly and simmer gently for two and one half hours. Add potatoes, carrots and tomatoes, continue cooking for an hour or until all is tender.

3
Lift meat from skillet and serve. If desired, make gravy by adding enough water to make two cups of liquid. Return to skillet and heat to boiling. Blend one tablespoon of flour with two tablespoons of cold water, stir this into boiling liquid and boil one minute, stirring constantly until thickened slightly.
Yield: eight servings.

BEEF

LORIN HOLLANDER

Mr. Hollander, a concert pianist who has appeared as guest artist several times with the National Symphony serves up a delicious Steak Tartare.

STEAK TARTARE

1 pound fresh, high quality, chopped beef
1 raw egg yolk
⅓ cup chopped onion
1 tablespoon chopped parsley
salt to taste

⅛ teaspoon paprika
1 tablespoon catsup
1 teaspoon Worcestershire sauce
1 teaspoon lemon juice
4 teaspoons hot (not "Chinese") mustard

Mix and serve with capers, raw onion, quartered lemon.
Yield: four servings as a first course.
Mr. Hollander suggests that for each additional pound of chopped beef, the same amount of the other ingredients should be added.

Joanna Simon

Joanna Simon sings mezzo-soprano with the New York City Opera.

STEAK TARTARE

2 eight ounce sirloin steaks
2 egg yolks
4 tablespoons olive oil
1 teaspoon French mustard
2 tablespoons onions, chopped
2 tablespoons gherkins, chopped

2 tablespoons capers
2 tablespoons parsley, minced
few drops wine vinegar
few drops Worcestershire sauce
salt
pepper

1
Trim excess fat from steaks and discard. Grind steaks coarsely in meat grinder and set it aside.

2
Place a medium-sized bowl in a larger one filled with cracked ice. (This will insure better results when making the mayonnaise.)

3
Put egg yolks in inner bowl, add mustard, salt and pepper and using a fork, start stirring with an even circular motion.

4
Drop by drop, add the olive oil and continue creaming the eggs until it becomes lightly-colored and thickened. To this smooth mayonnaise, add a few drops of vinegar and Worcestershire sauce.

5
Still stirring, blend in the onions, gherkins, capers and one and one-half teaspoons parsley.

6
Finally add the chopped steak and using two forks, blend it lightly but thoroughly in this tartare sauce.

7
Make a neat round of the meat on a serving dish and sprinkle remaining parsley as a garnish.
Yield: two servings.

BEEF

Cyril Ritchard

Mr. Ritchard, the incomparable gentleman actor has appeared in the Kennedy Center in the musical "Sugar" and directed the comedy "The Jockey Club Stakes."

STEAK AND WALNUTS

2 pounds good lean beef, cut into cubes
1 large onion, chopped
2 large tomatoes, coarsely chopped
salt
pepper
2 or 3 pickled walnuts
2 tablespoons of flour
vinegar from walnut can

1
Put cut up steak into casserole dish with onion, tomatoes, salt, pepper and walnuts.

2
Mix flour and vinegar, pour over other ingredients, cover and cook slowly in medium oven for at least three hours.

3
Just before serving, add a few more walnuts. If desired add carrots and potatoes when you put in the meat.
Yield: four servings.

Norman Treigle

Opera star Norman Treigle is a leading bass baritone with the New York City Opera. He has contributed the following recipe.

SUPREME BEEF KABOBS

2 pounds sirloin steak or sirloin tip roast cut in two-inch cubes.
¼ cup soy sauce
½ cup salad oil
1 teaspoon salt
½ teaspoon pepper

juice of whole lemon
¼ cup vinegar
2 whole cloves garlic
1 large onion, diced
1 large green pepper, seeded and diced

1

Marinate meat overnight in soy sauce, salad oil, salt, pepper, lemon juice, garlic, onion and green pepper.

2

Place meat, onion and green peppers alternately on skewers.

3

Cook under broiler or on barbecue grill about fifteen minutes, basting frequently. Serve with rice. Hot bread and green salad will complete the meal.

Yield: four servings.

Marilyn Horne

Metropolitan Opera Soprano and leading artist Marilyn Horne
has appeared in several concerts at the Kennedy Center .

SWEET-AND-SOUR MEAT AND BEAN DISH

5 strips bacon
2½ pounds ground beef
2 large onions, diced
2 cloves garlic, finely chopped
1 cup catsup
4 heaping tablespoons mustard
6 tablespoons vinegar
2 teaspoons salt
1 teaspoon black pepper

2 medium-sized cans Boston-style
baked beans, drained
2 medium-sized cans garbanzo
beans, drained
2 medium-sized cans dark-red
kidney beans, drained
2 to 3 tablespoons shredded
Cheddar cheese

1
Preheat oven to 350°. Fry the bacon in a large skillet until crisp;
remove and reserve drippings.
2
Combine ground beef, onion, green pepper, garlic and brown for a
few minutes in bacon drippings.
3
Mix catsup, mustard, brown sugar, vinegar into a sauce, then add to meat
mixture in skillet. Cook and stir for a few more minutes over low heat,
tasting and if necessary adding more of the above until
you get it the way you want.
4
Add the three kinds of beans. Mix well and transfer to a large casserole.
Place in oven for thirty minutes, or until it bubbles.
5
Remove, crumble the bacon all over the top with final topping of
Cheddar cheese. Place back in oven until cheese melts.
Yield: six servings generously.

Lamb

Jackie Coogan

Comedian Jackie Coogan entertained audiences at the Center in
"The Big Show of 1936," a multi-star show given during the Summer
of 1972.

BUTTERFLY LAMB

1 six or seven pound leg of lamb
Marinade:
2 medium onions liquified (or
grated, retaining juice)
2 cloves of garlic, crushed

1 bay leaf
salt
pepper
1 bottle inexpensive champagne

1
Have butcher debone and butterfly the lamb.
2
Marinate in refrigerator in the mixture listed above.
3
Start fire on outdoor grill an hour before cooking.
4
Wipe lamb clean, place fat side down on grill. Cover. Coals should be
at least 6" from meat. Cook thirty minutes. Turn, recover.
5
When done, lay butterfly on board. Cut in strips of three-fourths of an inch
thick. Serve with any style vegetable or potatoes.
Yield: six servings.

Sylvia Rosenberg

Sylvia Rosenberg is a concert violinist who has performed with the National Symphony at the Center. She writes that the dish below has the advantage that it can be prepared early enough that it won't interfere with the last minute rush prior to a concert. "I might add, as another advantage," she says, "that it can be conveniently forgotten when friends after a concert take you out to a good restaurant. . . ."

CASSEROLE A L'INDIENNE

1 leg of lamb, boned
2 large eggplants
1 can Italian tomatoes
6 cardamon seeds

salt
pepper
3 tablespoons oil

1
Cube the meat. Cube the eggplants (do not peel), sprinkle with salt and drain in a colander under a weight for one hour.
2
Saute eggplants in oil, add meat and tomatoes and spices. Cover and simmer gently for about one hour.
Yield: eight servings.

Charles Wadsworth

Mr. Wadsworth is Artistic Director and pianist of The Chamber Music Society of Lincoln Center. His wife writes the following about this recipe: "In 1966, after the Spoleto Festival in Italy at which Charles had directed his sixth annual series of noonday Chamber Music concerts, we were newlyweds, and took a week's visit to Paris. Wandering on the Isle St. Louis one beautiful summer day, we lunched in a tiny bistro. The lamb chops we had were delectable—and I have since concocted a version at home which reminds us of that day!"

LAMB CHOPS ROSÉ

8 one-inch lamb chops	2 tablespoons dried rosemary
6 shallots, sliced	salt
4 tablespoons butter	pepper
1 teaspoon cooking oil	juice of one lemon (approximately)
1 clove garlic, sliced	1 teaspoon flour
8 teaspoons dry mustard	½ cup rosé wine

1
Saute shallots and garlic in pan with one tablespoon butter and oil. Add salt.
2
Put one half teaspoon mustard on each side of chops. Put in frying pan over medium heat and sprinkle with rosemary. When brown turn over meat and repeat. Pour off fat and cook to taste (medium rare is best). Add freshly ground pepper and lemon juice and remove to hot platter.
3
Pour fat out of pan. Melt three tablespoons butter and mix with scrapings. Stir in flour, when mixture is blended, add wine. Stir and boil until smooth and serve over chops.
Yield: four servings.
Note: Serve with small white potatoes which can be sauteed in pan with meat (after being par-boiled). Canned whole small potatoes work very well.

Cynthia Gregory

Miss Gregory is a principle dancer with the American Ballet Theatre and writes the following comments about this recipe. "Although I am half Greek, I didn't get the recipe of this delicious Greek dish from a member of my family. A close friend of mine invited me to dinner and served this moussaka. It was one of the few Greek dishes I didn't know how to prepare, so I asked her for the recipe. It turned out to be one of my favorites."

MOUSSAKA

2 medium sized eggplants	¾ cup dry bread crumbs
1½ sticks butter	¼ teaspoon cinnamon
3½ teaspoons salt	¼ cup parsley, chopped
1½ cups onion, chopped	3 tablespoons flour
1½ pounds ground lamb or beef	3 cups hot milk
1 tablespoon tomato paste	1 cup ricotta or cottage cheese
⅓ cup dry red wine	2 eggs beaten
½ teaspoon fresh ground black pepper	⅛ teaspoon nutmeg
	¾ cup grated Parmesan cheese

1
Peel eggplant and cut into one-half inch thick slices. Melt four tablespoons butter in skillet; brown eggplant slices on both sides. Remove and sprinkle with one teaspoon of salt.
2
In same skillet melt four tablespoons of remaining butter. Saute the onions five minutes, add meat and cook five minutes, stirring frequently.
3
Stir in tomato paste, wine, pepper, cinnamon, parsley and one and one half teaspoons of remaining salt. Cook over low heat stirring frequently until mixture is fairly dry. Taste for seasoning. Cool.
4
Melt remaining butter in saucepan. Blend in flour and remaining salt. Add milk stirring steadily to the boiling point, then cook on lower flame five minutes longer.
5
Remove from heat, cool for five minutes, then mix in ricotta cheese, eggs and nutmeg.
6
Grease two-quart baking pan, dust lightly with breadcrumbs. Arrange layers of eggplant and meat, sprinkle each layer with breadcrumbs and Parmesan cheese. Start and end with eggplant.
7
Pour sauce over the top. Bake in preheated 375° oven one hour or until custard top is set and golden brown. Let stand thirty minutes at room temperature before cutting into squares.
Yield: four to six servings.

Potatoes and other Vegetables Pickles and Relishes

Daniel Heifetz

Daniel Heifetz is a concert violinist who craves potato Kugel and Kosher dill pickles. His grandmother's recipe for Potato Kugel is below.

POTATO KUGEL

3 pounds White Rose potatoes
8 eggs

½ teaspoon salt
2 tablespoons oil

1
Beat eggs and salt in mixing bowl and set aside.
2
Grate raw, pared potatoes over colander, allowing starch to drain. Lightly rinse with cold water. Squeeze out excess liquid.
3
Add potatoes to egg mixture. Mix well. Preheat empty greased casserole in 450 degree oven for just five minutes.
4
Fill casserole with potato mixture, cover and bake for one hour. Serve with choice of sour cream, gravy or applesauce.
Yield: six servings.

Mr. Schneider recommends his potato salad be served with his
Blood Sausage and Brains recipe which can be found in the
beef section of the Cookbook.

POTATO SALAD

4 pounds new potatoes   ½ cup good, light, olive oil
   (approximately)   wine vinegar
1 bunch chives   salt and pepper to taste.

1
Boil new potatoes with skin on. Take off skin while still hot and cut in half.
2
Put a lot of good, light, olive oil on top and let cool.
3
Add wine vinegar, salt and pepper to taste. Cut a bunch of chives on top.
4
Mix and serve cold.
Yield: eight servings.

Judith Blegen

Metropolitan Opera soprano Judith Blegen contributed the recipe below.

ASPARAGUS WITH ZABAGLIONE SAUCE

1½ pounds fresh asparagus
½ stick butter, melted
4 egg yolks

¼ teaspoon salt
8 tablespoons dry white wine
½ cup heavy cream

1
Snap off lower part of asparagus stems and discard. Wash stalks thoroughly and cook in salted water until tender about ten minutes. Pour butter over cooked asparagus.

2
Meanwhile combine egg yolks, salt, and wine in top of double boiler. Cook over hot, not boiling water until the mixture becomes thick. The mixture must be beaten continuously with a rotary beater.

3
Whip the cream and fold it into the mixture very gently.

4
Pour over asparagus-butter mixture and serve.
Yield: four servings.

Peter Serkin

Peter Serkin, the concert pianist, collected the Southwest Indian recipe below from *The Art of American Indian Cooking.*

BAKED VEGETABLES OF THE VINES

2 onions, peeled and chopped
2 cloves garlic, peeled and crushed
⅓ cup salad oil, plus 3 tablespoons
1 tablespoon salt
¼ teaspoon freshly ground black pepper
1 teaspoon oregano
¼ teaspoon cumin seed

¼ teaspoon powdered dill
2 cucumbers, zucchini or yellow squash, washed and sliced
1 large eggplant, washed and sliced
2 green peppers, washed, cored and sliced
2 tomatoes, washed, cored and sliced

1

In a flameproof oven casserole, saute onions and garlic in one-third cup salad oil until golden. Remove half the onions and set aside.

2

Mix together salt, pepper, oregano, cumin seed and dill.

3

Lay cucumbers on top of onion mixture in casserole; sprinkle with one-third of mixed seasonings and one tablespoon salad oil.

4

Add a layer of eggplant and sprinkle with one third of seasonings and one tablespoon of oil.

5

Add a layer of green peppers, then remaining herbs and one tablespoon of oil.

6

Cover casserole and bake for one hour in moderate oven (350 degrees).

7

Remove from oven, add layer of tomatoes, top with remaining onions; return to oven and bake uncovered for fifteen minutes more.

Yield: four to six servings.

Lorin Maazel

Lorin Maazel, the youthful conductor of the Cleveland Orchestra has performed over 3,000 concerts with major orchestras and taken seven world tours over the last twenty years.

GUACAMOLE DIP WITH TACOS

1 or 2 ripe avocados
1 tablespoon onion juice
2 tablespoons lemon juice
pulp of one tomato

1 scallion, finely chopped
½ teaspoon chili powder
1 teaspoon olive oil
½ teaspoon coriander

Mash avocados with silver fork, add remaining ingredients, chill and serve.
Yield: one or two cups.

Daniel Heifetz

KOSHER DILL PICKLES

12 medium cucumbers,   1 bunch fresh dill
    approximately three inches long   8 whole garlic cloves, peeled
 1 quart water   2 one quart jars
1½ tablespoon salt

1
Wash and drain cucumbers. Rinse dill.
2
On bottom of each jar, place one sprig of dill and two cloves of garlic.
Pack pickles into jars.
3
Mix salt and water and pour over pickles, covering them completely with
liquid. Top each jar with remainder of dill and two cloves of garlic.
4
Adjust covers and seal at once. Keep at room temperature six to eight days.
Refrigerate and use.
Yield: two quart jars.

Alan Titus

Alan Titus, the opera baritone, was the original celebrant in
Leonard Bernstein's "Mass."

CAPONATINA
(Sicilian Eggplant Relish)

1 large eggplant
salt
1 cup celery, diced
olive oil for frying
1 large onion, thinly sliced

½ cup Spanish olives, pitted and
sliced
2 tablespoons capers
2 tablespoons sugar
½ cup wine vinegar
1 cup tomato puree

1

Dice the eggplant, leaving skin on. Sprinkle with salt and place in a
colander. Place very heavy plate or skillet over the colander to press the
eggplant down. Let it stand this way for about an hour so the water will
drain from it. Pat the pieces dry with absorbent paper.

2

Simmer the celery in unsalted water to cover for ten minutes.
Reserve celery and water.

3

Slowly brown eggplant in the olive oil in a large, deep skillet. Put the
eggplant aside and lightly brown the onion in the same skillet; add the
olives, capers, sugar, the cooked celery with its liquid, and the eggplant.
Simmer for fifteen minutes, stirring occasionally.

4

Let the mixture cool. It can be stored in the refrigerator for at least a week.
With antipasto it is served on small crisp crackers.

Yield: eight servings.

A prize winning actress, Miss Harris was born in England and raised in India and Kashmir. She has played a variety of roles, which extend from Peter Pan to Ilyena in "Uncle Vanya" and appeared at the Center in Harold Pinter's "Old Times."

SQUASH SOUFFLE

2 pounds summer squash or zucchini
1 onion, grated
4 eggs, separated
3 tablespoons butter

3 tablespoons flour
1 cup milk
1 tablespoon sugar
1 teaspoon salt, or to taste
ground pepper to taste

1

Boil squash, mash and drain. Add grated onion and egg yolks well beaten.

2

Make sauce by melting butter, then add flour and stir, add milk and stir until it thickens. Add sugar, salt and pepper, then combine with squash mixture in large bowl.

3

Fold in stiffly beaten egg whites and pour all into baking or souffle dish and bake at 350° for forty minutes.

4

Serve at once if possible "but it doesn't matter if it goes flat . . . it tastes just as good!"

Yield: 4 to 5 servings.

roberta flack

Miss Roberta Flack has achieved world recognition for her unique
singing style, a combination of jazz, soul and pop.

SWEET POTATOES SUPREME

2 cups cooked mashed sweet
  potatoes
⅔ cup sugar
1 teaspoon cinnamon
½ teaspoon nutmeg
½ teaspoon mace

¼ teaspoon salt
¼ cup melted butter
2 eggs
1½ cups milk
½ to 1 cup raisins
marshmallows

1

Mix spice ingredients, eggs and milk, then melt butter in one and one half
quart casserole. Combine all ingredients, mixing well and pour into
greased casserole.

2

Bake thirty-five to forty minutes in a 350° to 375° oven. Remove from oven,
cover with marshmallows and return to oven for three to five minutes,
until marshmallows are lightly browned. Serve.

Yield: four to six servings.

Note: You can plump your raisins by letting them set in boiling water
fifteen to twenty minutes. Amount of water should be just enough to cover
raisins. Drain and add to sweet potato mixture.

Salads

SALADS

John Reardon

Metropolitan Opera baritone John Reardon often serves this endive salad instead of a green salad. It is good with any meat or fish dish.

ENDIVE SALAD

3 small Belgian endive heads
1 sixteen-ounce can of sliced beets
½ bunch watercress
2 tablespoons olive oil
1 tablespoon lemon juice or white wine vinegar
salt
pepper

1
With a sharp knife, cut endive crosswise into one half inch sections. Separate leaves, wash and drain thoroughly. Place in a bowl.

2
Remove hard stems from watercress and chop. Drain beets and cut slices in half. Add to endive.

3
Whisk together oil, lemon juice, salt and pepper; pour over salad and toss lightly.

Yield: four servings.

Peter Glenville

Peter Glenville, one of the most important and highly regarded directors on the Broadway and London stages, directed the new Tennessee Williams play "Out Cry" at the Kennedy Center.

SUMMER SALAD

1 can peach halves
1 cup mayonnaise
4 tablespoons tomato puree

½ pound fresh shrimp, cut up
lemon juice to taste

Mix lemon juice, tomato puree and mayonnaise, then fill peach halves with shrimp, pour mayonnaise over the whole, chill and serve.
Yield: four servings.

Breads

BREADS

Gil Evans

Jazz composer Gil Evans is also a Kennedy Center Founding Artist. He says the recipe below, which he received from a friend, is one of the best breads he has ever eaten.

JACK GREGG'S SOURDOUGH BREAD

Starter:

1 cup rye (or whole wheat) flour

1 tablespoon granulated yeast dissolved in three-fourths cup warm water

1
Mix ingredients, cover and keep at room temperature four or five days until sour.

Night before baking:

3 cups stone ground whole wheat flour

¾ cup water

1
Add ingredients to starter, cover and keep overnight at room temperature.

Baking:

3 cups whole wheat flour
¾ cup honey
3 tablespoons vegetable oil

1 cup water
2 teaspoons granulated yeast

1
Remove one cup of starter mixture for next baking.
2
Dissolve yeast in warm water allowing it to stand for fifteen minutes. Then add all ingredients to mixture adding yeast last. Stir until evenly mixed.
3
Knead and add more flour until dough is no longer sticky. Roll it into a ball.
4
Put it into a greased bowl and turn it over once. Cover and let rise in warm place for an hour.
5
Punch down dough to its original size and form into two loaves. Place on oiled cookie sheet or in bread pans. Cover and allow to rise another hour.
6
Bake at 375 degrees for forty-five to fifty minutes. When loaf is completely baked, it will give off a hollow sound when thumped and will come away from the sides of the pan and tumble out.
Yield: two loaves.

John Stewart

Mr. Stewart is a baritone with the New York City Opera. He writes, "This is the easiest bread recipe I know. It's delicious and will turn everyone off 'storebought.' "

BREAD

2 cups water
⅞ teaspoon salt
2 teaspoons honey
3 cups whole wheat flour
1 cup white flour (stone ground is best)

2 ounces crumbled yeast (follow directions for dry yeast on package if you can't find cake yeast)
1 tablespoon caraway seeds (optional)

1
Heat one-half cup water with salt and honey, then add remaining cold water, flour, yeast and caraway seeds. Put on wooden board.
2
Knead dough until it is more moist than rubbery, then allow to rise in two greased loaf tins in a warm spot for twenty minutes. Preheat oven to 425 degrees.
3
Bake forty minutes at 425-450 degrees. If desired, remove from tins after bread is done and brown for five minutes.
Yield: two loaves of bread.

Mr. DePreist, associate conductor of the National Symphony, says that the recipe below makes "one of the world's great joys and once you have made them at home you'll never eat them any other way." He adds, "you may not be able to stop at four, so make them the only meal of the day."

GLAZED YEAST DOUGHNUTS

⅞ cup milk
½ cup sugar
1¼ teaspoon salt
1 package granular yeast
¼ cup water
4¼ cups sifted flour
3 teaspoons nutmeg (the essential ingredient)

⅓ cup soft shortening
2 eggs
cooking oil

Glaze:
1½ cups sifted powdered sugar
3 tablespoons boiling water

1
Scald milk. Add sugar and salt. Allow to cool until lukewarm.
2
Sprinkle yeast over warm water. Stir until dissolved. Add milk mixture, *two* cups of flour and nutmeg. Beat well.
3
Stir in shortening, eggs and add remaining flour, kneading in final portion on a lightly floured surface.
4
Place in greased bowl (be sure top is greased) and allow dough to rise in warm place until doubled.
5
Turn out on lightly floured board. Roll dough one-third of an inch thick. Cut with doughnut cutter. Form trimmings into ball. When doubled roll out and cut.
6
Allow cut doughnuts to rise until light (about forty-five minutes). Leave uncovered so crust will form.
7
Using a floured pancake turner deftly transfer doughnuts into deep hot fat. Fry until golden brown, turning once. Drain.
8
Make glaze by combining sugar and water, then dip *slightly* cooled doughnuts into warm glaze.
9
Allow glaze to dry on doughnuts (placed on cake rack) and eat while still warm.
Yield: two dozen doughnuts.

Desserts

Eva Marie Saint

Miss Saint, an academy award winning actress, has appeared at the Kennedy Center in "Lincoln Mask" and "Summer and Smoke" with much critical acclaim. She says her recipe below is "sooooo easy to make!"

HEAVENLY APPLE PIE

1 cup sugar
1 cup flour
1 stick unsalted butter
3 Pippin apples

3 tablespoons lemon juice
1 cup cold water
2 tablespoons cinnamon

1
Grease glass pie plate and preheat oven to 350°.
2
Cut thin slices of Pippin apples and soak them in cold water and lemon juice at least ten minutes.
3
Knead butter and flour together, then add sugar to dough.
4
Spread one half dough in pie dish, add sliced apples and sprinkle with cinnamon.
5
Pat bits of remaining dough on top of apple slices, then bake in oven for one hour.
Yield: one pie.

Lucia Chase

Miss Chase is the Director (with Oliver Smith) of the American Ballet Theatre. She says that the recipe below "makes one of the lightest, most delicious cheesecakes I have ever eaten." We agree.

CHEESECAKE

4 cups zwieback crumbs	1½ pounds cottage cheese
8 tablespoons melted butter	2 tablespoons lemon rind
1 cup crushed pineapple	6 tablespoons lemon juice
4 tablespoons gelatin	2 cups heavy cream, whipped
6 egg yolks, lightly beaten	½ teaspoon salt
6 egg whites, stiffly beaten	¼ teaspoon cinnamon
1 cup sugar	¼ teaspoon nutmeg
1 cup pineapple juice	

1

Lightly toast zwieback crumbs in butter in small pan. Line sixteen inch mold with the buttered crumbs, reserving one half cup of crumbs. Spread crushed pineapple over top of crumbs.

2

Soak gelatin in small amount of cold water until dissolved.

3

Add sugar and pineapple juice to egg yolks. Cook slowly in top of double boiler until a thick custard. Add gelatin mixture to custard and cook, stirring, a few more minutes. Remove from stove.

4

Put cottage cheese through a strainer and add to custard. Add salt, lemon rind and lemon juice, cinnamon, whipped cream and beaten egg whites. Pour into crumb crust.

5

Sprinkle top of cake with reserved crumbs. Sprinkle with nutmeg. Chill overnight.

Yield: ten servings, generously.

Walter Eisenberg

Walter Eisenberg is the Music Director and Conductor of The Greater Boston Youth Symphony Orchestra.

CHERRY CHEESECAKE

2 eight-ounce packages cream cheese
½ cup sugar
1 teaspoon vanilla

3 eggs, well-beaten
1 graham cracker or vanilla wafer crust
cherry pie filling

1
Cream together cream cheese, sugar, vanilla and eggs; pour into pie crust.
2
Bake in 350 degree oven for about fifty minutes.
3
When cool, cover top with cherry pie filling.
Yield: eight servings.

Arlene Saunders

Opera Soprano Arlene Saunders from the Hamburg Opera was the Beatrix in Ginastera's "Beatrix Cenci" at the Center.

CHOCOLATE POPPY SEED TORTE

Torte recipe:
¼ cup butter or margarine
½ cup sugar
6 eggs, separated
½ cup fine bread crumbs

¼ pound semi-sweet chocolate, melted
⅓ cup ground poppy seeds
½ cup strawberry or apricot jam

1

Cream together butter and sugar. Beat egg whites until stiff but not dry. Beat egg yolks until thick and lemon-colored. Beat butter mixture and the crumbs into egg yolks.

2

Fold chocolate into the egg yolk mixture. Fold in the poppy seeds and the beaten egg whites.

3

Line two nine-inch greased layer pans with wax paper. Then spread batter into the pans evenly. Bake in oven for thirty minutes. Turn out cake and remove the paper at once.

4

The layers may be put together with jam. Then cover the top and sides with Chocolate Frosting (recipe below).

Frosting:
8 one-ounce squares semi-sweet chocolate
¾ cup sugar

¾ cup water
1 tablespoon butter or margarine

Combine first three ingredients and cook to soft ball stage (234 to 236 degrees). Remove from heat. Add butter. Beat and frost the cake.
Yield: one nine-inch layer cake.

Patrick Hayes

Patrick Hayes brings great talent to the Washington area as Managing Director of The Washington Performing Arts Society.

CURRIED FRUIT BAKE

⅓ cup butter or margarine
¾ cup brown sugar, packed
4 teaspoons curry powder
1 No. 1 can pear halves

1 No. 1 can cling peach halves
1 No. 1 can pineapple (slices or chunks)

1
Preheat oven to 325 degrees.
2
Melt butter, add sugar and curry.
3
Drain, dry fruit; place in one and one-half quart casserole; add butter mixture and bake for one hour.
Note: May be made a day ahead and reheated. Almost any combination of canned fruits may be used and proportions varied.
Yield: six servings.

Mary Costa

Mary Costa is an opera star who also performs in films. She appeared in Washington at the Kennedy Center production of "Candide." Miss Costa's mother writes that the recipe below was named for her daughter by the chef of the St. Francis Hotel in San Francisco who created it for her.

COSTA DE ORO

1 cup fresh raspberries
1 cup sliced peaches

2 ounces Kirsch
3 ounces Triple Sec

1
Mix all ingredients together and heat until raspberries begin to lose their juice, giving the liqueurs a light purple color.
2
Flame and serve at the table by candlelight.
Yield: two servings.

Natalie Hinderas

Natalie Hinderas the famous concert pianist, writes of the tradition behind the recipe below: "Each year, on the weekend before Christmas, my husband, my daughter, and I plan our annual 'Carol Sing'. We started this tradition nearly a decade ago when we agreed Christmas should be more than just rushing, buying, and gift giving. So, we began to have our friends come to our home and spend an evening enjoying each other's talents, singing some familiar and some seldom-heard carols and reading the story of the birth of the Child that gave hope to the world. When the songs are sung, stories read and musical offerings complete, I serve a supper of chili, salad and this favorite-of-all fruit cakes to end our joyous evening."

CHRISTMAS FRUIT CAKE

2 cups mixed candied fruit, chopped
1 cup restored, dried apricots, chopped
1 cup restored, dried prunes, chopped
1 cup candied pineapple, chopped
1 cup light raisins
1 cup strawberry or apricot preserves
1½ cup currants
1 teaspoon vanilla

1½ cups dark raisins
½ to ¾ cup cognac or light rum
1 cup pecans, coarsely chopped
1 cup walnuts, coarsely chopped
6 eggs
1 cup dark brown sugar
1 cup butter
2 cups flour
½ teaspoon nutmeg
½ teaspoon cloves
2 teaspoon cinnamon
1 teaspoon instant coffee

Soak all the fruit, preserves, vanilla, and liqueur in a large glass bowl for approximately eighteen hours.

2

When fruits are ready, grease and lightly flour three nine by five by three loaf pans. Set oven at 300 degrees. Add nuts to bowl containing fruit.

3

Cream butter, flour and spices, beating into a light, fluffy mixture. Beat eggs and sugar together until thick and fluffy. Stir egg mixture thoroughly into creamed butter-flour mixture.

4

Carefully pour batter over fruit and nuts in the large bowl. Mix gently and quickly to cover fruit with batter.

5

Fill prepared pans two-thirds full. Pat down firmly to remove any air bubbles. Cover each pan with aluminum foil to seal.

6

Bake cakes in preheated oven two hours. Remove foil and then bake forty-five minutes longer, or until top of each cake is browned.

7

When completely cooled, turn out of the pans. Wrap each in rum or cognac -soaked cloth and then in foil. Store in airtight box for at least two weeks. If storing longer, sprinkle with liqueur.

Yield: three cakes.

DESSERTS

Paul Hill

Paul Hill is the conductor of the Paul Hill Chorale. His hobby is baking "probably because I worked in a bakery during two years of college" and he serves the dish below to the Chorale at Christmas parties. He warns that the finished ring "contains about ten thousand calories per square inch!"

FESTIVE HOLIDAY RING

Combine in large bowl:
3 cups all-purpose flour
1 cup whole wheat flour (or fourth cup all-purpose flour)
½ cup powdered dry milk
1 egg
¼ cup honey
4 tablespoons cooking oil

1 teaspoon salt

Combine in small, warmed bowl:
1 cup (approximately) warm water
2 packages dry yeast
½ teaspoon butter flavoring
½ teaspoon almond flavoring
½ teaspoon lemon flavoring

1
Combine large and small bowls and stir well. It should be quite stiff but still moist. (Only practice will indicate the exact consistency.)

2
Turn out on floured board and knead well. Dust with flour if still too wet. (Knead fifteen to twenty minutes; the length of kneading makes the dough smoother.) Place in greased bowl, turning once to grease surface. Cover and let rise until double; punch down, let rise twenty more minutes.

3
Divide dough in half, prepare half at a time. Roll each to a rectangle about three-eighths to one half-inch thick. Spread with a filling.*

4
Roll, starting from long side, like a jelly roll. Shape in a ring on greased baking sheet. With scissors cut almost through at one inch intervals. Pull sections apart and overlap by twisting. Let rise thirty minutes. Then bake at 375 degrees about twenty-five minutes.

5
Ice with glaze made of confectioner's sugar and very little hot water. Dot with nuts, cherries or other colorful fruit.

Filling: make a choice of one listed below or create one of your own.

Melted butter, sugar cinnamon, raisins, nuts.

Brown sugar and butter.

Citron and sugar.

Prune whip spread.

Canned fruit, well drained and cut into small pieces the size of fruit cocktail.

Mincemeat and sugar.
Yield: about two dozen servings.

DESSERTS

Maurice Abravanel

Maurice Abravanel, Music Director and Conductor of the Utah Symphony, has been a guest conductor at the Kennedy Center.

GATEAU LUCIE

4 dozen lady fingers
10 eggs, separated
1 package (8 squares) Baker's semi-sweet chocolate
½ teaspoon instant coffee
1 teaspoon sugar

2 tablespoons water
1 pint vanilla ice cream
½ pint whipping cream
½ teaspoon vanilla extract
sugar

1
Butter a two-quart mold. Line bottom and sides of mold with lady fingers (about three dozen).
2
Melt chocolate in top of double boiler. While chocolate is melting, beat egg whites until stiff. Add instant coffee, sugar and water to chocolate and remove from heat.
3
Add slightly-beaten egg yolks to chocolate mixture and blend well. Fold egg whites into chocolate mixture and immediately pour into lined mold. Place remaining lady fingers on top.
4
Chill in refrigerator for at least six hours or overnight.
5
Two hours before serving, remove ice cream from freezer and place in refrigerator to melt.
6
One hour before serving, place mold in two inches of hot water for one minute. Pass knife around sides of mold to loosen. Put large, slightly shallow serving plate in mold and turn upside down.
7
Pour melted or almost melted vanilla ice cream over cake. Let soak in refrigerator for one hour. With spoon, coat sides from time to time with melted ice cream.
8
Whip cream, adding vanilla and sugar to taste and garnish cake with puffs of whipped cream.
Yield: eight to ten servings.

Mr. Fairbanks, a master actor who brought elegance and charm to the stage
in the Kennedy Center's production of "The Pleasure of His Company,"
writes that the elegant recipe below was produced by his wife "as the best
I can do for myself is a 'Dagwood sandwich' or a boiled egg."

MARRON MERINGUES

3 meringues* in shape of
  a pie crust
2 tins puree marrons

2 pints heavy cream, whipped
whole marrons (or crisp slivers of
  toasted unsalted almonds)

1
Let meringues cool, then put a layer of puree marrons, then a layer of
unsweetened whipped cream. Do the same thing for each layer
including the top layer.
2
Cover the entire combination with more whipped cream (as in a cake).
3
Before serving decorate the top with either whole marrons or crisp slivers
of toasted unsalted almonds.
Yield: eight servings.

*Meringue recipe (makes three seven-inch meringues)
6 egg whites, room temperature
¼ teaspoon cream of tartar
¼ teaspoon salt

2 cups *very fine* sugar
2 teaspoons vanilla extract

1
Start beating egg whites at moderately slow speed until they are foaming
but still soft; then beat in cream of tartar and salt; gradually increase
speed to moderately fast; as soon as they hold shape softly beat in one-fourth
cup sugar; beat for thirty seconds then add one-fourth cup sugar and
so on until the cup has been beaten in.
2
Beat in vanilla, then beat at fast speed two to three minutes until eggs are
very stiff. Immediately begin sprinkling slowly second cup of sugar
in eggs and fold with spatula.
3
Heat oven to 250 degrees. Butter and lightly flour two baking sheets,
then draw three circles of about seven-inch diameter each with your fingers.
Pour meringue mixture in pastry bag and squeeze onto circles until each
one is about three-eighths of an inch high. Flatten each with spatula.
4
Place in upper half or upper third of oven and immediately turn oven down
to 200 degrees. Bake one hour regulating heat so that meringues
don't color.

Dominic Cossa

Metropolitan opera baritone Dominic Cossa tells this story about his fabulous chocolate mousse:
"Some years ago while appearing in Oklahoma City, I went to a famous restaurant and had a superb dinner. Dessert consisted of an exquisite chocolate mousse. I returned several times, and in vain tried to obtain the recipe from the head waiter with whom I had gotten on speaking terms. "Years later, again in Oklahoma City, I visited this restaurant, and again enjoyed the chocolate mousse, and again tried and failed to obtain the recipe. That same evening, while waiting in the wings for an entrance cue, I struck up a conversation with a pleasant, rotund gentleman who had been locally engaged to sing a small part in the production. I could hardly believe my ears when upon discussing occupations he told me he was the 'chef' at my favorite restaurant. In fact, he himself had made the mousse. The next day I had the recipe."

MOUSSE AU CHOCOLATE

1 cup sugar	½ cup egg yolks
6 tablespoons white corn syrup	1 cup egg whites
¼ cup water	1½ cups heavy cream, stiffly
15 ounces sweet German	whipped
chocolate	chopped pistachio nuts (optional)
¼ pound unsalted butter	

1
Melt chocolate and butter in top of double boiler.
2
Cook sugar, syrup and water until it will spin an eight-inch thread.
There should be about one-half cup of syrup.
3
Beat egg yolks until thick and lemon-colored. Slowly pour the hot syrup into the yolks and continue beating. Then add cooled, melted chocolate to the mixture.
4
Beat egg whites to stiff peaks and fold into chocolate mixture. Place in a stainless steel bowl and allow to set about two hours in refrigerator.
5
Remove from refrigerator and add one cup of the stiffly whipped cream.
Beat furiously until a fluffy, creamy mass of rich chocolate.
6
Decorate with remaining whipped cream and garnish with nuts.
Yield: eight servings.

PINCHAS ZUKERMAN

Mr. Zukerman, although still in his twenties, is one of the most prominent violinists of our time. He describes the recipe below as "a nice, light, tempting, fattening—but fun—after-concert feast."

PANCAKE À LA PINK

½ cup flour
2 eggs
½ cup milk
pinch nutmeg

½ cup butter
2 tablespoons confectioner's sugar
juice of one half lemon

1
Mix flour, eggs, milk and nutmeg—leave lumpy. Preheat oven to 425 degrees.
2
Melt butter in a large, oven-proof frying pan until bubbly and pour batter into this.
3
Bake for fifteen or twenty minutes or until golden brown. Sprinkle with powdered sugar, then squeeze lemon juice over it.
4
Serve at once with lingonberry preserves and a bottle of champagne.
Yield: four servings.

Johanna Meier

Johanna Meier is a soprano with the New York City Opera.

PFANNEKUCHEN
(Paper-thin Pancakes)

5 eggs, at room temperature
5 tablespoons sugar
2 cups heavy cream, at room temperature
2 cups milk, at room temperature
6-7 tablespoons cake flour
1 teaspoon salt

1 stick sweet butter, melted
1 lemon or orange, grated
1 eight-ounce jar apricot or strawberry jam
½ cup powdered sugar
2 teaspoons Grand Marnier

1
Beat eggs and sugar until frosty. Add one cup of cream and beat well. Add milk and beat. Sift flour into liquid. Add salt, cooled melted butter and the gratings.
2
Cover and let stand at least one hour in a warm place.
3
Butter iron skillet. Then pour about one tablespoon of butter into skillet for each pancake. Each pancake should be as thin as possible. Cook on both sides.
4
Place two teaspoons of jam into the center of each pancake and roll. Dust lightly with sugar and serve with whipped cream. Yield: about fifteen pancakes.

Tony Roberts

Mr. Roberts, a versatile and well-known film actor appeared in Washington in the premier production of 'Sugar,' the musical version of "Some Like It Hot." He writes about his recipe "I would suggest you never make less than two of these at a time; one for five or six friends and the other for yourself. If all you've got is one—you'll never share it with anybody!"

RUM CAKE A LA SUAVE

½ cup pecans chopped
1 eighteen ounce package Duncan Hines Butter Recipe Golden Cake Mix
1 package vanilla instant pudding mix

½ cup dark rum
½ cup water
½ cup vegetable cooking oil
4 eggs

(Note: Do *not* follow box directions on cake mix or pudding!)

1
Crumble nuts into Bundt pan which has been greased. Preheat oven to 350°.
2
Mix dry ingredients in large bowl and add rum, water, oil, and eggs. Mix for two minutes. Pour batter into pan and bake for fifty minutes.
3
Immediately pour glaze on cake. Cool thirty minutes before removing from pan.

Glaze:
1 cup sugar
1 stick butter

¼ cup rum
¼ cup water

1
Put ingredients in sauce pan and boil for two or three minutes. Save a little of the glaze to pour on the cake after it has been removed from the pan. Glaze should be reheated when this is done.
Yield: ten servings.

Terry Orr

Terry Orr is one of the principle dancers with the American Ballet Theatre and he says the recipe below "was always one of my favorite desserts, which my mother served preferably after a light meal."

RUM CREAM PIE

1 cup chocolate cookies,
  crumbled with rolling pin
1 stick butter, softened
6 egg yolks (or four eggs)

1 scant cup sugar
1 package unflavored gelatin
½ cup dark rum

1
Make a crumb pie shell of rolled chocolate cookies and butter.
Reserve a few dry crumbs for top of cream filling.

2
Beat egg yolks until light, then add sugar. Meanwhile, soak gelatin in water, then put gelatin and water over a low flame, bring to boil and pour it over the sugar-egg mixture, stirring briskly.

3
Fold whipped cream into egg mixture and flavor the whole combination with the rum. Chill and serve.
Yield: 8 servings.

Itzhak Perlman

Mr. Perlman is a famous violinist who has given us a delicious recipe. He writes 'the first recipe that comes to mind is not mine. As a matter of fact, the first time I ate it was at the home of Danny Kaye. I liked it so much that I use it very often. I hope it is not too complex, but even if it is, it is worth it. It is very delicious."

BASIC SOUFFLE OMELETTE

2 eggs, separated
1 tablespoon butter
2 to 3 teaspoons granulated sugar

shot of brandy
shot of Grand Marnier

1
Beat egg whites until foamy, add one to two teaspoons of sugar. Continue beating until peaks appear, not overly stiff.
2
Beat yolks with same amount of sugar until lemon-colored. Light broiler.
3
Fold yolks into whites. Heat omelette pan and heat butter over medium flame until bubbly. Pour egg mixture into pan, constantly stirring pan so that omelette does not stick.
4
Just as omelette begins to solidify put under broiler flame so it can rise (about fifteen or twenty seconds). As it becomes golden brown, remove from pan and tilt carefully into a large plate. Carefully fold omelette in half without breaking.
5
While omelette is being cooled, heat liqueurs so that when omelette is ready, flaming mixture can be poured over it.
Yield: two servings.
Note: The omelette can be served with preserves, such as apricot or strawberry. This filling should then be put on the omelette before it is folded over.

Max Rudolf

Conductor Max Rudolf writes the following about his tempting recipe:
"When the Pierre Monteuxs came over from Hancock to Mount Desert,
Maine, to have lunch with the Rudolfs, the nut roll was served and enjoyed
tremendously by Maître Monteux. Noticing that his host, who was on a diet,
declined, he turned to Mrs. Rudolf and remarked gravely 'Madame, zeez eez
raison for divorce.'"

VIENNESE NUT ROLL

½ cup sugar, granulated
4 eggs, separated
4 ounces ground walnuts (or pecans)

½ pint heavy cream, whipped
4 tablespoons powdered sugar

1
Beat egg yolks with granulated sugar, add stiffly beaten egg whites and
ground walnuts.
2
Spread mixture on buttered and floured wax paper on a large baking sheet.
Bake in 350 degree oven for fifteen to eighteen minutes.
3
When cooled, spread whipped cream, to which two tablespoons of
confectioner's sugar has been added, over dough. Then roll and top with
remaining powdered sugar. Refrigerate several hours before serving.
Yield: eight servings.

DESSERTS

(signature)

Mr. Menuhin, the famed violinist, says about his recipe, "After the above experiment, the kitchen was in such a mess that the family were obliged to live on ice cream for the next three days."

WHOLE TREE ICE CREAM

1 cup heavy cream, whipped
1 tablespoon maple syrup
1 tablespoon pure honey
1 ounce almonds, lightly roasted and ground
1 tablespoon freshly ground strong coffee

pinch of powdered ginger
pinch of cinnamon
dash of Jamaica rum
3 to 4 egg yolks, beaten until creamy
2 ounces bitter chocolate, grated

1
Combine all the ingredients in large bowl then pour into loaf tin or ice trays.
2
Freeze at least three hours in freezer.
Yield: four to five servings.

Cookies and Candies

COOKIES AND CANDIES

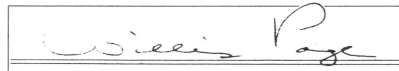

Mr. Page is the Conductor and Music Director of the Jacksonville Symphony.
He says Penuche is his favorite candy and this recipe is terrific!

PENUCHE

2 cups light brown sugar
¾ cup milk
¾ cup chopped pecans or walnuts

1 teaspoon vanilla
2 tablespoons butter

1
Blend sugar and milk over low heat. Continue stirring until mixture
begins to boil and boil without stirring until mixture forms a soft ball
when dropped into cold water.

2
Remove from heat. Add butter, vanilla and nuts.

3
Cool. When cool, beat vigorously until mixture thickens. Then pour into
a greased cake pan and let harden to fudge consistency.
Yield: two dozen squares of fudge (depending on size of square).

Royez Fernandez

Royes Fernandez, a principal dancer with the American Ballet Theatre, was born and raised in New Orleans where he first tasted this recipe.

PRALINES

1 cup white sugar
1 cup brown sugar
½ cup cream

2 tablespoons butter
1½ cups pecans
1 tablespoon sherry or brandy

1
Dissolve sugars in cream in medium sauce pan. Bring to a boil over low heat and continue boiling, stirring constantly, until candy thermometer registers 228 degrees.

2
Add butter and pecans; stir to combine, and continue cooking without further stirring until syrup registers 236 degrees or forms a soft ball in water.

3
Remove from heat, add sherry or brandy and beat with wooden spoon until slightly thickened but still glossy.

4
Drop by tablespoons onto waxed paper. If mixture begins to harden while turning out, place over hot water.

5
When cool, wrap patties individually in plastic wrap for storing. ·
Yield: several dozen.

Menus and Recipes

Mrs. Dwight D. Eisenhower

MENU FOR BUFFET SUPPER AFTER THE CONCERT

A menu with recipes contributed by Mrs. Dwight D. Eisenhower, wife of the thirty-fourth President of the United States.

Cold Curry Soup*
Chicken Jewel Ring Salad*
Frosted Mint Delight*
Toasted English Muffins

RECIPE FOR COLD CURRY SOUP

⅓ cup butter
¼ cup onion, minced
¼ cup celery, diced
1½ teaspoons curry powder
1 teaspoon salt

⅛ teaspoon pepper
¼ cup flour
1 quart milk
2 chicken bouillon cubes
flaked coconut

1
Melt butter in saucepan over low heat. Saute onions and celery in butter until transparent.
2
Blend in seasonings and flour. Add milk, stirring constantly. Cook until smooth and thickened.
3
Add bouillon cubes; stir until blended. Chill thoroughly.
4
Pour into chilled bowls and sprinkle with flaked coconut.
Yield: six servings.
*recipe included

RECIPE FOR CHICKEN JEWEL RING SALAD

Cranberry layer:

1 envelope unflavored gelatin
1 cup cranberry juice cocktail

1 can (or 1 pound) whole cranberry sauce
2 tablespoons lemon juice

Chicken layer:

1 envelope unflavored gelatin
¾ cup cold water
1 tablespoon soy sauce
1 cup mayonnaise

1½ cups diced cooked chicken
½ cup diced celery
¼ cup coarsely chopped almonds, toasted

1

Sprinkle one envelope of gelatin in cranberry juice cocktail in saucepan to soften. Place over low heat, stirring constantly, until gelatin is dissolved. Break up whole cranberry sauce; stir into gelatin mixture and lemon juice. Turn into six-cup ring mold; chill until almost firm.

2

Sprinkle second envelope of gelatin on cold water in saucepan to soften. Place over low heat, stirring constantly, until gelatin is dissolved. Remove from heat; stir in soy sauce. Cool. Gradually stir into mayonnaise until blended. Mix in remaining ingredients. Spoon on top of almost firm cranberry layer. Chill until firm. Unmold on salad greens.

Yield: eight servings.

RECIPE FOR FROSTED MINT DELIGHT

2 one-pound cans crushed pineapple with juice
¾ cup pure mint-flavored apple jelly

1 pint whipping cream
2 teaspoons confectioner's sugar
1 package gelatin

1

Have all ingredients chilled.

2

Melt the jelly and mix the crushed pineapple into it.

3

Dissolve the package of gelatin in one cup of the juice from the pineapple. Mix the gelatin mixture into the jelly mixture.

4

Whip the cream, sweeten it with the sugar, and fold it into the mixture. Put into the freezer until firm. Do not freeze solid.

Yield: ten to twelve servings.

Mrs. Lyndon B. Johnson

PICNIC LUNCH BEFORE THE MATINEE

A menu with recipe contributed by Mrs. Lyndon B. Johnson for a Picnic
for her four grandchildren before a Kennedy Center Matinee.
Since Mrs. Johnson's grandchildren like smorgasbord eating, "Nini"
as they call her, packed a little of a lot of things.
Fried Chicken Drumsticks
Finger Sandwiches
Crisp Garden Vegetables (see note)
Peppermint Straws 'n Oranges*
Moon Rocks*
Strawberry Milk Shakes
Mrs. Johnson packed three kinds of finger sandwiches: pimento cheese,
tuna fish and peanut butter and jelly. The crisp vegetables were sprinkled with
seasoning salt and packed in little individual containers. She served the
milk shakes in miniature fruit jars.
*Note: These were included because all grandmothers think children
should eat them, not because children like them.*

PEPPERMINT STRAWS 'N ORANGES

Roll one medium-sized naval orange to soften, being careful not to break
the skin. Cut a hole in the top just large enough to insert one peppermint
stick. Be sure the candy is the porous "sugar" variety to permit sipping
the juice.

MOON ROCKS
(cookies)

1½ cups sugar	1 cup coconut
3 eggs	1 level teaspoon soda
1 scant cup butter	pinch salt
4 cups flour	1 teaspoon cloves
½ cup corn syrup	1 teaspoon cinnamon
1 cup pecans	1 teaspoon allspice
1 cup raisins	1 teaspoon nutmeg

1
Sift flour with soda, pinch salt, cloves, cinnamon, allspice and nutmeg.
2
Cream butter and sugar. Add eggs, one at a time, and beat after
each addition.
3
Add syrup, then stir in flour. Add pecans, raisins and coconut.
4
Drop by teaspoonfuls onto greased cookie sheet and bake in 375-400
degrees oven until lightly brown. Children love them.
Yield: several dozen.

Mrs. Alice Roosevelt Longworth

TEA AFTER THE MATINEE

A menu with recipes contributed by Mrs. Alice Roosevelt Longworth,
daughter of President Theodore Roosevelt, the widow of Speaker of The
House Nicholas Longworth and *duenna* of Washington.
Bread and butter*
Lots of homemade sugar cookies*
Earl Grey's Jacksons of Piccadilly Tea

BREAD AND BUTTER

Buy very good unsliced bread; butter it with sweet butter, then cut it into
very thin slices with a very sharp knife and repeat.

SUGAR COOKIES

2 sticks butter (or one stick
  butter, one stick margarine)
1 cup sugar
1 egg
1½ cups flour, sifted

½ teaspoon salt
½ teaspoon vanilla
Grated coconut or cinnamon and
  sugar or grated orange peel

1
Cream butter and sugar and add unbeaten egg. Beat well and add flour,
sifted again with salt, gradually. Blend well. Add vanilla.
2
Drop by teaspoonful onto lightly greased cookie sheet.
3
Press with fork prongs and sprinkle with lightly toasted coconut, or
cinnamon and sugar, or grated orange peel. (If you want them very flat
and thin, lightly grease bottom of glass, dip in sugar mixture and
use it to flatten each cookie.
4
Bake in a 375 degree oven for twelve to fifteen minutes, then remove from
the pan with a spatula.
Yield: about four dozen cookies.

Mrs. Richard M. Nixon

DINNER BEFORE THE OPERA OR BALLET

The menu with recipes below was contributed by Mrs. Richard M. Nixon, wife of the thirty-seventh President of the United States.

Baked Oysters White House
Paillettes Dorees

Supreme of Duckling Bigarade*
Wild Rice Amandine
Asparagus Tips Au Beurre

Bibb Lettuce Salad
Bel Paese Cheese

Strawberry Mousse*

ROAST DUCKLING BIGARADE

1 five and one-half pound dressed duckling with trimmings and giblets
4 naval oranges
3 tablespoons sugar
¼ cup wine vinegar
2 small onions, peeled
2 small carrots, peeled
4 cups water

1 teaspoon salt
2 tablespoons Curacao
2 tablespoons arrowroot
juice of ½ lemon
1 bouquet garni (the white part of 1 leek and 1 stalk of celery cut into about 4 inch pieces and tied with string)
pinch of white pepper

1
Prepare the duck stock in the following manner: chop up the giblets and trimmings, onions and carrots and brown them in the oil in a saucepan. Drain off the oil, add the water, salt, and bouquet garni. Simmer for one and a half hours, then strain stock.

2
Cut the orange part of the orange peel into tiny slivers about one inch long. Blanch in boiling water for fifteen minutes and dry. Season the inside of the duckling, add one-third of the orange peel and truss. Brown duckling in 425 degree oven for twenty minutes, then lower the heat to 350 degrees, turning the duck on one side for thirty-five minutes and the other side for thirty minutes. Skim the fat from the bottom of the pan from time to time. If the duckling is not brown put it to an upright position and roast for fifteen minutes more.

3

To make the sauce: boil sugar and vinegar over a medium flame until it becomes a dark brown syrup. Remove from the heat and pour in one-fourth of the prepared stock. Simmer and stir until syrup is dissolved.

4

Mix the arrowroot with three tablespoons of wine, then add the remaining stock and the arrowroot mixture to the hot sauce. Stir in the orange peel and simmer for three to four minutes. Check the seasoning and keep hot.

5

Remove the white skin from the oranges, cut them in slices and set aside.

6

Place the duck on a heated platter and keep hot. Skim all fat from the roasting juice and add the remaining wine and boil, reducing to about three tablespoons. Strain into the sauce and simmer. Stir in the Curacao. If the sauce seems too sweet, add a few drops of lemon juice. Garnish platter with orange slices and pour over some of the sauce. Serve the rest in a gravy boat.

Yield: six servings.

STRAWBERRY MOUSSE

½ ounce gelatin	1½ pints fresh strawberries
¼ cup cold water	1 cup confectioner's sugar
½ cup hot water	1½ cups heavy cream—whipped
juice of ½ lemon	1 tablespoon Kirschwasser

1

Put in blender a little less than one pint strawberries, lemon juice, sugar and Kirschwasser and cold water. Blend ingredients until well pureed.

2

Dissolve gelatin in hot water and mix together with the strawberry puree.

3

Whip cream stiff in a stainless steel bowl.

4

As soon as the strawberry puree thickens, fold it into the whipped cream (use rubber spatula for this purpose) and then put the mousse into one quart dessert form. Chill for several hours.

5

To unmold, dip form in hot water (three to four seconds) and reverse onto a china or glass platter. Decorate strawberry mousse with strawberries and whipped cream.

Yield: six servings or one quart.

Mrs. Aristotle Onassis

EARLY DINNER BEFORE THE CONCERT

An elegant menu with recipe contributed by Mrs. Aristotle Onassis
Risotto with mushrooms*
Cold sliced veal and paté de foie gras in aspic
Salad of endive and Bibb lettuce
Lemon ice in tall cylindrical mould with mint leaves on top
Very thin sugar cookies

RISOTTO WITH MUSHROOMS

½ cup butter
¼ cup beef marrow
1 onion, finely chopped
1½ cups fresh mushrooms, sliced
2 cups rice

3 cups beef stock
salt
pepper
freshly grated Parmesan cheese

1
Melt one-fourth cup butter in an earthenware casserole, add beef marrow and onion and cook until the onion colors. Add sliced mushrooms and cook for five minutes.
2
Add two cups of rice and cook, stirring constantly, until rice begins to take on color. Pour in three cups hot beef stock, salt and pepper to taste.
3
Mix all together well and simmer the rice, stirring from time to time, for twenty to twenty-five minutes until the liquid is absorbed and the rice is tender.
4
Just before serving sprinkle the risotto generously with freshly grated Parmesan cheese and remaining butter.
Yield: eight servings.

POULTRY

Chamber Music Chicken Wings, 66
Cherry Chicken Surprise, 67
Chicken with Almonds, 68
Chicken Breasts Piquant, 69
Chicken Breasts with Sour Cream
and Brandy, 70
Chicken with Crumbs, 71
Chicken Jewel Ring Salad, 167
Chicken Livers Holbrook, 72
Chicken in Sherry Wine, 73
Cuban Chicken Fricassee, 74
Hungarian Creamed Chicken, 75
Pollo Mole, 76
Poulet Cocotte à la McCoo, 77
Smothered Chicken and
String Bean Dinner, 78
Tallulah's Chicken, 79
Roast Duckling Bigarade, 170
Rock Cornish Hens, 80

HAM AND PORK

Beer-glazed Ham, 82
Fruited Ham, 83
Apricot-Raisin Pork Chops, 84
Chinese Pork with Spinach, 85
Pork Chop Casserole, 86
Opera Spareribs, 87

VEAL

Osso Buco (Italian Veal Stew), 90
Roast Loin of Veal, 91
Veal Parmigiana, 92

BEEF, BEEF STEWS AND CASSEROLES

Beefsteak Woronoff, 94
Beef Curry, 95
Beef Stew, 96
Blood Sausage and Brains, 97
Brazilian Beans, Meat and Rice, 98
French Beef and Vegetable Casserole, 99
Golabki (Polish stuffed cabbage), 100
Goulash, 101
Hong Kong Rice, 102
Marinated Flank Steak, 103
Mushrooms and Meatballs, 104
Pot Roast with Wine and Olives, 105
Steak Tartare , 106 , 107
Steak and Walnuts, 108
Supreme Beef Kabobs, 109
Sweet and Sour Meat and Bean Dish, 110

COOKIES AND CANDIES

MENUS AND RECIPES

Notes

Notes

Notes

Notes

Notes

Notes

Notes

Notes

Notes

Notes

Notes

Notes